The

A working tool of management

Wallace Clark

Alpha Editions

This edition published in 2019

ISBN : 9789389525106

Design and Setting By
Alpha Editions
email - alphaedis@gmail.com

THE GANTT CHART

A WORKING TOOL OF MANAGEMENT

By

WALLACE CLARK

Member, American Society of Mechanical
Engineers ; Taylor Society

WITH APPENDICES
by
WALTER N. POLAKOV
and
FRANK W. TRABOLD

NEW YORK
THE RONALD PRESS COMPANY
1922

PREFACE

In 1917, after a careful inspection of certain factories in which Mr. H. L. Gantt had installed his methods, General William Crozier, then Chief of Ordnance, retained Mr. Gantt to act in a consulting capacity on production, first at the Frankford Arsenal, and then, immediately after the declaration of war, in the Ordnance Department at Washington.

Large orders had been placed with arsenals and other manufacturing plants for the production of arms and munitions, but it was difficult to get a comprehensive idea of what progress was being made in the filling of these orders. Quantities had suddenly jumped from hundreds to millions, and it was impossible to convey by means of typewritten tables the significance of such unusual quantities or the time necessary to produce them. Charts of the usual type were unsatisfactory because they did not sufficiently emphasize the time and because of their bulk, since only one item could be put on a sheet.

Mr. Gantt concentrated his attention on the development of a method of charting which would show a comparison between performance and promises. Several years previous to this time, he had used a chart on which the work for machines was "laid out" according to the time required to do it. The Gantt Progress Chart, as developed from this early form, was found to help in the making of definite plans and to be highly effective in getting those plans executed. The rate at

which the work goes forward is continuously compared
with the advance of time, which induces action to ac-
celerate or retard that rate. These charts are not static
records of the past—they deal with the present and
future and their only connection with the past is with
respect to its effect upon the future.

General Crozier quickly grasped the possibilities of
this chart in helping to fix responsibility for action or
lack of action and had it introduced in various branches
of the Ordnance Department. During 1918 these
charts were used in the United States arsenals, in the
production of naval aircraft, and in other government
work, such as that of the Emergency Fleet, the Shipping Board, etc.

After the Armistice Mr. Gantt resumed his private
consulting practice. With these charts, which provided
a new method of presenting facts, he was able to re-
verse the usual way of installing production methods
and to build up a system of management which could be
understood not only by every individual connected with
the management, but by the workmen as well. This
marked a new era in the usefulness of the management
engineer.

Mr. Gantt never made any attempt to patent or
copyright his charts. He not only gave samples to anyone who asked for them, but published them in several
magazine articles and as illustrations to his book on "Organizing for Work." He was always glad to have other
people make use of his knowledge.

Since Mr. Gantt's death, November 23, 1919, there
has been an increasingly earnest desire on the part of
workmen, managers, and owners of industrial plants to

get at the facts in regard to the operation of their industries, to measure the effectiveness of management, and to secure fair play for both workman and owner. Because the Gantt chart, wherever it has been used, has been of such great value as a means to attain these ends and because the author believes that in its development Mr. Gantt has rendered an undying service to industry, it is here presented in such a way as to make it available for more general use.

At the beginning of the book the principle of the Gantt chart is stated, especially the feature which distinguishes it from all other charts, namely: Work planned and work done are shown in the same space in their relation to each other and in their relation to time.

The technique of drawing the charts is explained fully, not with the idea of confining the reader to any rigid rules but to give him the result of years of experience in the development of the charts to their present state, so that it will not be necessary for him to go over the same ground. This technique has been worked out with the purpose in view of making it easy to draw the chart and easy to read it correctly, that is, to understand readily the action which should be taken.

The application of the chart to the various classes of work in the usual industrial plant is outlined and the possibilities of a much broader application are suggested.

Collectively the charts show whether or not equipment is being used at any given time and, if not, the reasons for idleness; fix responsibility for idleness and are effective in preventing it; show how the work of individual employees compares with a standard of performance and emphasize the reasons for failure, thus fixing the responsibility for the removal of those obstacles; enable the work to be readily planned so as to make the best possible use of available equipment and to get work done when it is wanted. These charts show the load of work planned for a whole plant or an entire industry, give a continuous comparison of performance with schedule, and make it possible for an executive to foresee future happenings with considerable accuracy and to overcome obstacles more easily.

In the chapter on the American Merchant Marine an outline is given of the application of the various types of Gantt charts to the solution of an exceedingly complicated problem which arose during the Great War.

In conclusion, the effects of the use of these charts are outlined briefly. Although they are only lines drawn on paper, where they are used production is increased, costs and inventories are reduced, special privilege is eliminated, initiative is stimulated, an organization is built up of men who "know," and workmen become interested in their work.

In the Appendix Mr. Frank W. Trabold has given his experience as to "How a Manager Uses Gantt Charts" and Mr. Walter N. Polakov, in "The Measurement of Human Work," has explained the philosophic concept behind these charts.

The reader should not get the idea that this book presents a complete method of management; it merely presents a part of such a method, that is, the part played by the Gantt chart in solving specific problems, in getting at the facts in any situation, and in presenting those facts so that they will be understood in their relation to time.

There is perhaps no limit to the application of these charts. They have been successfully used in both small and large businesses, ranging from automobile painting shops, employing two or three men, to nation-wide industries. They have been used in storekeeping, all kinds of office work, foundries, drop forge shops, textile mills, printing and publishing plants, machine shops, power plants, public service corporations, shipbuilding, and many other kinds of work.

The author wishes to acknowledge help in the preparation of this book, which has been so generously given by Messrs. Walter N. Polakov, Frank W. Trabold, Fred J. Miller, George M. Forrest, Howard A. Lincoln, George H. Rowe, Karl G. Karsten, William E. Camp, and by Leon P. Alford, who suggested the series of articles on "The Gantt Chart" for *Management Engineering,* from which this book has been developed.

Above all, the author wishes to acknowledge his indebtedness to Mr. H. L. Gantt. He placed service to others before profit to himself. It was such men as Gantt that Woodrow Wilson had in mind when he said: "All that saves the world is the little handful of disinterested men that are in it."

WALLACE CLARK.

New York City,
April 10, 1922.

CONTENTS

LIST OF ILLUSTRATIONS

THE GANTT CHART

CHAPTER I

THE PRINCIPLE OF THE GANTT CHART

An Aid to Management

Management is concerned almost entirely with the future. Its task is to decide on policies and to take action in accordance with those policies which will bring about a desired condition. Decisions which affect the future must be based on a knowledge of what has happened in the past, and while a record that certain events have taken place or that a certain amount of work has been done is of value in making such decisions, it does not give us sufficient insight into the future. We must know *when* those events took place or the *rate at which* the work was done. In other words, the *relation of facts to time* must be made clear.

If management is to direct satisfactorily the operation of our industries under conditions of ever-increasing difficulty, its decisions and its actions must be based not only on carefully proved facts but also on a full appreciation of the importance of the momentum of those facts. *The Gantt chart, because of its presentation of facts in their relation to time, is the most notable contribution to the art of management made in this generation.*

The Advantages of the Gantt Chart

The use of a Gantt chart makes it necessary to have a plan. Recording that plan on a chart where it can be seen by others has a tendency to make it definite and accurate and to promote the assignment of clear-cut tasks to individuals. The plan is presented so clearly on these charts that it can be understood in detail and as a whole not only by the executive himself but also by those above him and by his subordinates.

The Gantt chart compares what is done with what was done—it keeps the executive advised as to the progress made in the execution of his plan, and if the progress is not satisfactory it tells the reasons why. The executive's time is thus saved because each time a figure is received he does not need to compare it with past records and decide whether it is good or bad. He has determined once for all what figures will be satisfactory and has recorded them on the chart. The comparison of the accomplishment with the plan then becomes merely a clerical task and the executive is left free to study the tendencies and take the action indicated by the chart.

The Gantt chart emphasizes the reasons why performance falls short of the plan and thus fixes the responsibility for the success or failure of a plan. Causes and effects with their relation to time are brought out so clearly that it becomes possible for the executive to foresee future happenings with considerable accuracy.

The Gantt chart is, moreover, remarkably compact. Information can be concentrated on a single sheet which would require 37 different sheets if shown on the usual type of curve charts. There is a continuity in the Gantt chart which emphasizes any break in records or any lack of knowledge as to what has taken place.

The Gantt chart is easy to draw. No drafting experience is necessary, for only straight lines are used. The principle is so simple that anyone with average intelligence can be trained to make these charts.

Gantt charts are easy to read; no lines cross each other and all records move with time across the sheet from left to right. Charts drawn in pencil or black ink convey an impression of practicability, simplicity, economy, and strength which it is not possible to obtain by the use of colored inks or even squared paper. Since no colors need be used on Gantt charts, prints are as intelligible and effective as originals.

The Gantt chart visualizes the passing of time and thereby helps to reduce idleness and waste of time.

The Gantt chart presents facts in their relation to time and is, therefore, dynamic. The chart itself becomes the moving force for action.[1]

The Principle of the Chart

In the Gantt chart a division of space represents both an amount of time and an amount of work to be done in that time. Lines drawn horizontally through that space show the relation of the amount of work actually done in that time to the amount scheduled. This is the feature which distinguishes the Gantt chart from all other charts. Equal divisions of space on a single horizontal line represent at the same time:

1. Equal divisions of time.
2. Varying amounts of work scheduled.
3. Varying amounts of work done.

---

[1] The word "dynamic" is used in its popular sense. "Kinetic" would be more exact.

Thus it shows the relation of time spent to work done. Furthermore, since *knowledge of what has happened and when it happened causes action,* the past projects itself into the future and records charted in this way become dynamic. A single example may make this method clear.

A week's work is planned as follows:

Monday..........100
Tuesday..........125
Wednesday 150
Thursday..........150
Friday.... ..... .150

A sheet is ruled with equal spaces representing days (Figure 1) and the amount of work planned is shown by figures on the left side of the day's space. So far the chart shows the schedule and its relation to time.

FIGURE 1. GANTT CHART SHOWING THE DAILY SCHEDULE

The work actually done through the week was:

Monday.......... 75
Tuesday..........100
Wednesday 150
Thursday..........180
Friday.......... 75

This is charted as shown in Figure 2.

Lines are drawn through the daily spaces to show a comparison between the schedule and the actual accomplishment. On Monday the space represents 100; only 75 were done, so a light line is drawn through 75 per cent of the space. On Tuesday 125 were planned; 100 were done; a line is therefore drawn through 80

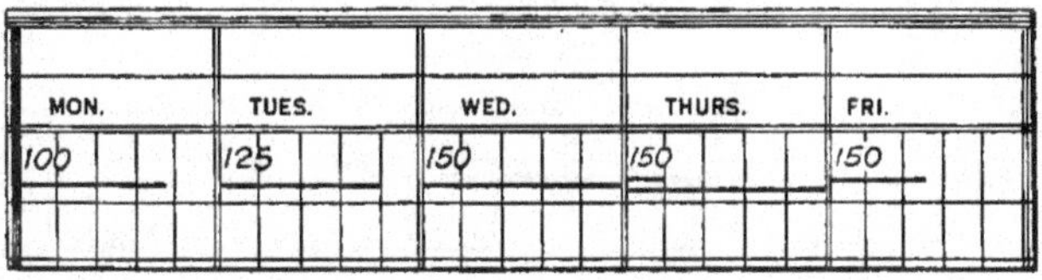

FIGURE 2. GANTT CHART SHOWING THE WORK
ACTUALLY ACCOMPLISHED

per cent of the space. On Wednesday 150 were to be done and 150 were done, so the line is drawn through the entire space. On Thursday 150 were scheduled and 180 were done, i.e., 120 per cent of the schedule; a line is therefore drawn all the way across the space to represent 100 per cent and an additional line through 20 per cent of the space. On Friday 150 were planned, but only 75 were done; a line is accordingly drawn through 50 per cent of the space. The chart now gives a comparison day by day of the amount of work done and the amount scheduled and the relation of both schedule and accomplishment to time.

It is, however, desirable to know how the whole week's work compares with the schedule and so the figures representing the *cumulative schedule* are entered on the right of the daily space (Figure 3). At the end of the day on Friday, for instance, the total amount to be done up to that time was 675. A heavy line is therefore drawn to show a comparison between the *cumulative work done* and the *cumulative schedule*. On

Monday the heavy line is the same length as the light line. Of the 100 done on Tuesday, 25 have to go to make up the shortage for Monday. The remaining 75 are applied on Tuesday's schedule and the heavy line

FIGURE 3. GANTT CHART SHOWING THE CUMULATIVE SCHEDULE AND THE CUMULATIVE WORK DONE

is drawn through 60 per cent of the Tuesday space. Of the 150 done on Wednesday, 50 are needed to meet the schedule to Tuesday night and the remaining 100 are applied on Wednesday's schedule of 150, the line being drawn through 66 per cent of the space. Of the 180 done on Thursday, 50 are used to meet the schedule to Wednesday night and the line representing the remaining 130 is drawn through 87 per cent of the day's space. Of the 75 done on Friday, 20 go to meet the schedule to Thursday night, leaving 55 to be applied to Friday. The cumulative line, therefore, shows us that on Friday night the work is two-thirds of a day behind the schedule.

This chart (Figure 3) shows the relation of the schedule to time, the work done each day in relation both to time and the schedule, and finally the cumulative work done and its relation to time and the schedule.

CHAPTER II

HOW TO DRAW A GANTT CHART

The Sheet on which the Chart is Drawn

Size

Gantt charts can, of course, be drawn on paper of any size or shape. It has been found, however, that the most satisfactory size is 11 x 17, because when records are charted by months there is ample space for a complete year, and when they are charted by days, two weeks can be shown on one sheet. A sheet 11 x 17 is also a standard size for binders, and when folded once to 8½ x 11 it can be placed in a standard letter file.

Paper

If no copies of charts are needed or they are to be photostated, it is possible to use any kind or weight of paper, although bond paper 16 pounds in weight is possibly most satisfactory. When charts are to be kept a number of years, 28-pound bond or ledger paper may be used.

If blueprints of charts are desired, bond paper without any water-mark should be used, because on a blueprint a water-mark will sometimes show up as prominently as the lines drawn on the chart. The weight of the paper determines the time necessary to make the blueprint, i.e., the heavier the paper the longer it takes for the light to penetrate it. When paper is

9

very light in weight, it crinkles and soils easily. The best results are, therefore, obtained by using a medium weight—say, 12 or 13 pounds.

Binding

It has been found more satisfactory to bind these sheets on the right rather than the left, for two reasons:

1. Records charted naturally move with time from left to right. This puts the index at the outer edge of the binder and makes it easy to find a specific item in a book of charts.

2. When the time shown on one sheet has passed, a sheet without indices is placed on top of it. In this way the weeks or months are built up on top of each other with only one index. (See Figure 4.)

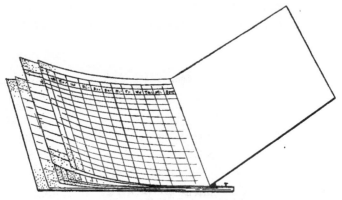

FIGURE 4.   BINDER FOR CHARTS

Perpendicular Ruling

First lay off from the right side of the sheet a binding edge of not less than 2 inches.

From the left side of the sheet lay off a space in

which to write the necessary description of the work to be charted. This space may vary in width, but it has been found that one column 2 inches wide and another $\frac{1}{2}$ inch wide will serve most purposes. In some cases, still another column $\frac{1}{2}$ inch wide has been added.

The space remaining between the binding edge and the indexing space is divided into columns representing units of time, i.e., hours, days, weeks, months, years, etc. If the hours of the day are to be shown, the space is divided into two parts, each representing a week. Each half is then divided into the days of the week and each day into the working hours of the day. (See Figure 5a.)

If days and weeks are to be shown, divide this space into ten equal parts for weeks and subdivide those spaces into five, six, or seven narrow columns, according to the number of days per week during which work is to be done. (See Figure 5b.)

If months are to be shown, divide the space into twelve columns for months and subdivide each month into five columns, each representing 20 per cent of the month's total. (See Figure 5c.) Separate days, weeks, and months by heavy lines or by double or triple lines.

Use black ink for ruling chart forms, since gray or colored inks are not so readily blueprinted or photographed.

Horizontal Ruling

From the top of the sheet lay off a space 2/3 inch high in which to write a description of the information contained on the sheet. Under that lay off another space 2/3 inch high in which to print or write the units of time

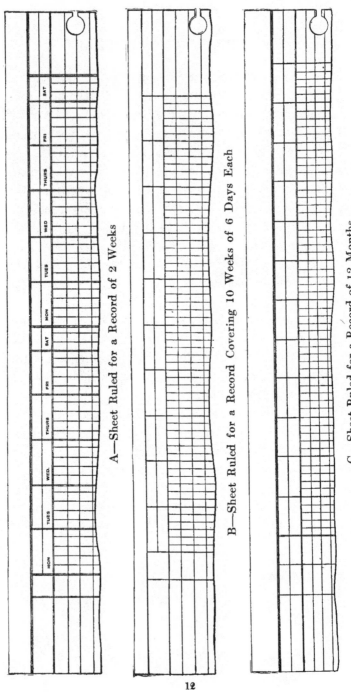

A—Sheet Ruled for a Record of 2 Weeks

B—Sheet Ruled for a Record Covering 10 Weeks of 6 Days Each

C—Sheet Ruled for a Record of 12 Months

FIGURE 5. STANDARD RULED SHEETS USED IN PLOTTING GANTT CHARTS

and dates. Above and below this space use double or heavy lines. (See Figure 5a.)

Through the remaining space rule horizontal lines three to the inch, which is double typewriter spacing for standard Pica type. This spacing is also considered the best for written records. See that the first line on which records are to be entered is typewriter spacing (multiple of 1/3 inch) from the top edge of the sheet. It will then be possible to insert the sheet in the typewriter and turn the cylinder until the writing point is brought to any desired line without adjustment by means of the variable line spacer.

Where charts are not to be typed and it is desirable to get as much information on a sheet as possible, the horizontal lines can be ruled four to the inch.

Printing the Form

These forms may be either printed or machine-ruled, the quantity required determining which method is the more economical.

If any type is used on the form, such as the days of the week or the form name, Gothic type should be used. Since all the lines in the letters of that style of type are of equal weight, the type matter will be readable when blueprinted or photostated.

DRAWING THE CHART

Entering the Schedule[1]

At the top of the sheet enter a description of the information to be charted on the sheet, placing at the

---

[1] Entering the schedule, and other information expressed in words or figures, can he done more economically on a typewriter than by hand. The charts used as illustrations in this book are lettered by hand in order to make the cuts clearer.

extreme left the one or two words which distinguish this sheet from others in the same binder.

At the heads of the columns representing units of time enter the dates.

In the columns on the left side of the sheet write a description of the work to be charted on the various lines.

The date or hour when work is to be begun is indicated by a right angle opening to the right thus:

$$\lceil$$

The date on which work is to be completed is indicated by an angle opening to the left, thus:

$$\rceil$$

The amount of work scheduled for any period of time is indicated by a figure placed at the left side of a space, thus:

$$\big|10 \qquad \big|$$

The amount of work to be done up to any specified time is indicated by a figure placed at the right side of a space, thus:

$$\big| \qquad 40\big|$$

If these entries are made by hand, use India ink so that good blueprints can be made. If they are type-written, use a heavily inked black record ribbon and place a sheet of carbon face up against the back of the paper. The resulting blueprints will show clear white typing.

Entering Work Done

Light lines represent work done during any given period of time.

The length of the line bears the same relation to the width of the space as the amount of work done bears to the amount scheduled.

Heavy lines represent the cumulative amount of work done and show its relation to the amount scheduled to be done up to any given date.

When charts are drawn in shops, where they are for immediate use and do not need to be kept for reference, they are drawn up in lead pencil.

If charts are to be kept for future reference or are to be reproduced, India ink is used. Light lines can be drawn with a sharp pen point or a drawing pen; heavy lines are most easily drawn with lettering pens (Figure 6).

FIGURE 6. LETTERING PEN USED FOR MAKING GANTT
CHARTS

Size O, which is 1/16 inch wide, is the best for individual cumulative lines, while size 1, which is ⅛ inch wide, is used for group totals.

No colors need be used on Gantt charts because lines representing different things never cross each other and can be clearly described in words in the left margin. Whatever emphasis is desirable, as in the case of lines representing totals, can be secured by varying weights of lines. The use of black ink has the same advantage mentioned in connection with lines printed in black, in that blueprints or photostat copies are as legible as the original charts.

CHAPTER III

THE APPLICATION AND USE OF THE GANTT CHART

Three Classes of Charts

The principle of the Gantt chart can be applied to any human activity, but up to the present time it has been applied most extensively to industrial production. Even in that field there are great possibilities for its further application, but the Gantt charts used up to date fall into three general classes:

1. Man and Machine Record Charts.
2. Layout and Load Charts.
3. Progress Charts.

In the Man and Machine Record Charts, Gantt provides a mechanism to show the relation between what is done and what could be done by a man or a machine. The gap between actual and possible accomplishment is idleness, that is, the neglect to make any use of time or a proper use of it.

The Machine Record Chart shows when a machine is not made use of and the reason why. The Man Record Chart shows whether or not a man makes a proper use of his working hours, and if not, it indicates the reason why.

The reasons for idleness, which are emphasized by the Man and Machine Record Charts, indicate that steps must be taken some time in advance in order to avoid idleness. The Layout Chart is Gantt's mechanism to plan work so as to avoid idleness of men and equipment and to get work done in the order of its importance. The Load Chart shows the amount of work, in hours or days, ahead of a plant or any part of a plant.

The executing of a plan is of equal importance with the making of that plan. The Progress Chart is Gantt's mechanism to get work done by showing a comparison of the accomplishment with the plan and the reasons for failure to live up to that plan.

The Gantt chart simplifies a complex situation or problem and points to the action which should be taken.

The Broad Field for the Gantt Chart

The value and adaptability of these charts is recognized by all progressive engineers. In an article on "Routing Considered as a Function of Up-To-Date Management," H. K. Hathaway, industrial engineer, says:

> For continuous flow production such as this I know of nothing better for recording output and comparing performance with capacity or what ought to be produced, than the straight line charts developed by Mr. H. L. Gantt, which show required and actual production in terms of both quantity and time. Their use, however, is not limited to the class of work just described.

In his book, "Organizing for Work," Gantt quoted a letter which shows the broad applicability of his chart. This letter was dated December, 1917, and written by Dean Herman Schneider of the University of Cincinnati to General C. B. Wheeler, then Chief of Ordnance

Referring to the Gantt charts in use in the Ordnance Department, he said:

> Each production section has production and progress chart systems. . . . The charts give a picture of the progress of the whole Ordnance program including lags and the causes therefor. Combined in one office and kept up to date, they would show the requirements as to workers, . . . materials, transportation, accessory machinery and all the factors which make or break the program.
>
> . . . Finally, these charts assembled in one clearing office would give the data necessary in order to make the whole program of war production move with fair uniformity, without disastrous competition and with justice to the workers.

Use During the War

About six months before Dean Schneider's letter, Colonel (later General) John T. Thompson, then in charge of the Small Arms Division, had adopted these charts with enthusiasm. At the end of the war he received the Distinguished Service Medal "for exceptionally meritorious and conspicuous service as Chief of Small Arms Division of the office of Chief of Ordnance, in which capacity he was charged with the design and production of all small arms and ammunition thereby supplied to the U. S. Army, which results he achieved with such signal success that serviceable rifles and ample ammunition therefor were at all times available for all troops ready to receive and use them."

When this medal was awarded to General Thompson, he sent a copy to Mr. Gantt with the following generous word of appreciation:

A large share in this reward for the accomplishment of a
great war task is due to H. L. Gantt and his assistants.
The Gantt general control production chart was my compass.

In the leading editorial in *Industrial Management*
for February, 1918, entitled "Master Control of American Industries for War—Man or Method?" **L. P.**
Alford said:

How are we to obtain master control of the efforts of
these millions of people who are engaged, or to be engaged,
in manufacturing, of the production equipment that they
operate, of the business organizations of the country?—in
short, how are we to control the industry of the United
States? This question is the most critical one facing the
American people today. Tied up in it are all the problems
of transportation, mining, shipbuilding, war industries, and
the production of everything needed to care for our civilian
population during the war. . . .

The solution of this problem involves the complete organizing of American industry, both that part engaged in producing war materials and supplies and the other part turning
out articles for civilian consumption. Once organized, all of
this industry must be coordinated, so that its efforts will
be directed to the production of those things needed by the
Government in the quantities demanded by the needs of war
—and no more—and beyond that for such civilian needs as
are most pressing, for not all of the latter can be satisfied.
This demands a form of control far different from anything
that has been looked forward to in this country. It is more
proper to ask for the way in which this form of master control might be set up. Fortunately, a suggestion is at hand
based upon work already done. . . .

Plot all of the Government requirements of materials of
every kind on Gantt charts, together with the receipts of all
this material. That is, bring under graphic analysis all of
the facts in regard to the production of Government material
necessary to give managerial control.

Measuring Efficiency of Industry

Another engineer, Walter N. Polakov, in a paper on "Principles of Industrial Philosophy," presented at the annual meeting of the American Society of Mechanical Engineers, December, 1920, said:

> The achievement of Gantt offers a means of measuring the human or social efficiency of industry. . . . Gantt's method has made it possible to ascertain the cause of the diseased industry just as blood analysis established the cause of malaria. While the latter made the completion of the Panama Canal possible, the former will transform industry from servitude into creative service and its pensioners into respectable members of the community. . . .
>
> Unlike statistical diagrams, curve records, and similar *static* forms of presenting facts of the past (Gantt) charts . . . . are *kinetic*, moving, and project through time the integral elements of service rendered in the past toward the goal in the future.

CHAPTER IV

THE MACHINE RECORD CHART

Drawing the Machine Record Chart

The purpose of the Machine Record Chart is to show whether or not machines or equipment are being used and, if not, the reasons for idleness.

In a manufacturing plant the foreman uses a sheet ruled to represent the working hours of his shop or department. If he works an 8-hour day, he has each wide column which represents a day ruled off into four narrower columns, each representing 2 hours. If he works a 9-hour day, he rules the day off into four wide spaces of 2 hours each and one narrower space for 1 hour (Figures 7 and 8).

On the left side of this sheet the foreman or his assistant lists all the machines, benches, or work spaces in his department, arranging them in groups according to responsibility, if there are any subforemen. If there are no subforemen, the foreman arranges them by kinds of machines. At the top of each group he leaves a space for the total of that group and at the top of the sheet a line for the total of the department (Figure 7).

Opposite each machine number the foreman indicates whether or not the machine has been running by drawing a light line across the space to indicate how many hours the machines ran. The ratio of the line to the space is the same as the ratio of the hours the machine ran to the working hours of the plant. A blank space indicates that the machine did not run, and in that space a letter or symbol is placed to indicate the reason why. The letter indicating the reason is placed at the beginning of the space representing the idleness, so that it would be bisected by the light line if the line were continued, thus:

The fewer the symbols used, the easier it is to get men to understand them and use the chart.

Under the light line a heavy line is drawn to indicate the cumulative running time of the machine for the whole week. The length of this heavy line is always equal to the sum of the light lines for the various days. The heavy line rests on the printed line and the light line is drawn about 1.10 inch above the top of the heavy line.

The running time of the individual machines in a group is averaged and the light and heavy lines entered for the group total. In the same way the groups are averaged to get the total running time of the shop, and the lines are drawn at the top of the sheet (Figure 7).

Keys should be attached to charts the first two or three times they are given to anyone. When the charts are thoroughly understood, the keys may be discontinued or kept for reference in the binder in which the charts are placed.

It is better not to send charts regularly to men who have not the authority to act on them. They may get the impression that the charts are merely cleverly drawn records rather than facts so presented as to indicate the action which should be taken.

	June 13 MON.	14 TUES.	15 WED.	16 THURS.	17 FRI.	18 SAT.	20 MON.	21 TUES.	22 WED.	23 THURS.	24 FRI.	25 SAT.

Total Operating Time of Machines in Dept.

Drill Presses Total

- 1401
- 1344
- 623
- 869
- 373
- 858
- 1343
- 1333
- 1325
- 1336
- 1071

Milling Machines Total

- 1259
- 528
- 477
- 273

Broaching Mach. Total

- 1436
- 1198
- 1378

FIGURE 7. A GANTT MACHINE RECORD CHART

LEGEND

| | Width of daily space represents working hours of the plant. |

Time machine was running.

Weekly total of individual machine.

Weekly total of group of machines.

Weekly total of all machines in department.

The portion of the daily space through which no line is drawn represents the time the machine was idle.

In order to prevent future idleness, it is necessary to know the reasons for the idleness which has occurred in the past so that responsibility can be fixed. Therefore, wherever there is no line on the chart, a letter is entered in the space to indicate the reason for idleness.

REASONS FOR IDLENESS

E—Waiting for set-up.   P—Lack of power.
H—Lack of help.   R—Repairs.
M—Lack of material.   T—Lack of tools.
O—Lack of orders.   V—Holiday.

When there is more than one reason for idleness, the reason entered on the chart is determined by asking questions in the following order:

R—Is the machine ready to run?
O—Is there an order for the machine?
M—Is there material ready to be worked on?
T—Are there tools?
P—Is there power to run the machine?
H—Is there an operator for the machine?

Circumstances sometimes change the relative importance of the reasons for idleness and it is then necessary to change the sequence of these questions.

25

FORGE DEPARTMENT

PRODUCTIVE MACHINES SHEET NO.3

NOVEMBER HOLIDAY

		MON. 3	TUES. 4	WED. 5	THURS. 6	FRI. 7	SAT. 8	MON. 10	TUES. 11	WED. 12	THURS. 13	FRI. 14	SAT. 15
Total 1500 lb. Hammer (Continued)	327	O		O	O	O	O	O	O	O	O	O	O
	664	O		O	O	O	O	O	O	O	O		O
	676						H		T				R
	695	R		R	R	R	R	R	R	R	R		
Total 2000 lb. Hammer Total	303	V			O		O	O	O	O	N	N	N
	308							O			O	O	O
	331	R			R			O	O	O	O	O	O
Total 3000 lb. Hammer Total		V		R	R	R	R	R	R	R	R		R
	646	R		T	T			T	T R				
	696	O						O		O			O
	697												
	698												
	700												
Total Steam Hammer Total		N	V	N	N	N	N	N	N	N	N		N
600 lb.	340	O		O	O	O	O	O	O	O	O	O	O
800 lb.	291	O			O	O	O	O	O	O	O	O	O
Total Upsetters Total		V											
No. 3 "	245						T	T	T	T	T	R	R
No. 2 "	290	T						T				T	
No. 1 "	5005												
Total Trip Hammer,		N	V	N	N	N	N	N	N	N	N		N

FIGURE 8. MACHINE RECORD CHART OF DROP FORGE HAMMERS

This is the third sheet of a Machine Record Chart of drop forge hammers. Although the groups of hammers shown were running at less than 50 per cent capacity, that is not an unusual amount of idleness, even under normal conditions. This chart was drawn in 1919, when business conditions were good and the capacity of the hammers of certain sizes was booked several months in advance. In spite of that fact, some of these hammers were idle for lack of orders (indicated by O).

The chart called attention to the fact that it would be advisable for the sales department to make a persistent effort to secure orders for those hammers which were out of work rather than to spend their time going after orders for hammers which were already loaded to capacity for several months.

Repairs (indicated by R) are frequently necessary to hammers on account of the nature of the work, but the chart indicated that these repairs kept the hammers non-productive for an unnecessarily long time.

Idleness due to lack of tools (indicated by T) was rather frequent. The tools in this case were dies used in making the forgings, and a good deal of idleness of hammers was caused by the fact that the dies had not been completed by the die-sinkers or because the dies had broken.

This chart constantly kept before the foreman and superintendent the obstacles which prevented them from running their shop at full capacity and helped to fix the responsibility for idleness.

27

Using the Chart

In the Machine Record Chart the foreman has a graphic record of the running of his machines which enables him to visualize his problem and to grasp the facts and the tendencies much more firmly than he could from any written record or from watching the machines. Moreover, the chart emphasizes above everything else the reasons for the idleness of machines, and those reasons indicate very clearly who is responsible for the idleness.

Since it is the foreman's aim to get work done, he studies the facts shown and translates the chart into action. He eliminates as much as possible of the idleness over which he or his subordinates have control. If machines have been "waiting for set-up," he plans the work of his set-up men more carefully, and, if necessary, trains an additional set-up man. If machines are idle for "repairs," he does all he can to push the completion of the repairs. If the trouble is "lack of material," he asks the storekeeper for help.

A considerable part of the idleness of machines appears to be due to causes over which the foreman has no control, so he takes the matter up with his immediate superior, who may possibly be the superintendent. He shows the charts to him and asks for his assistance in avoiding further idleness.

If machines are down for "lack of help," the superintendent discusses the matter with the employment department and finds out what prevents the securing of the kind of workmen needed.

If idleness is due to "lack of tools," the superintendent takes the matter up with the foreman of the toolroom; if due to "lack of power," he finds out whether or not it would be wise to provide for auxiliary power service.

If the trouble is "lack of orders," the superintendent takes it up with the sales department to see that he is manufacturing what can be sold or that the salesmen are provided with information in regard to the product which will enable them to sell it.

Summary of Idleness

In order to get a better idea of the progress made in the running of his machines, the foreman prepares a Summary of Idleness Chart on which he enters each week the one line which summarizes his whole department and he shows the hours of idleness due to the various reasons (Figure 9). When machine rates have been developed to show the actual cost of idleness, he uses dollars and cents on the chart instead of hours.

The foreman in whose office these charts are kept not only advances his own interests by keeping them, since they enable him to become a more important and capable man in the eyes of the management and his workmen, but by the same means he calls to the attention of other individuals their responsibilities in regard to keeping the shop busy.

The Machine Record Charts are of great value to the superintendent because they bring to his attention the problems on which his help is most needed. He does not have to go around the shop asking his foremen what is wrong and frequently finding out only when it is too late. The obstacles which prevent his foremen from keeping their machines running are brought to his atten-

PRODUCTIVE MACHINES Week Ending	PER CENT OF CAPACITY USED	TOTAL HOURS OF IDLENESS	DETAILS OF IDLENESS HOURS DUE TO							
			LACK OF HELP	LACK OF MATERIAL	LACK OF ORDERS	LACK OF POWER	REPAIRS	LACK OF TOOLS	WAITING FOR SET-UP	HOLIDAY
Week Ending July 5th		1972	236	302	29	0	381	178	62	784
" 12		1478	259	436	250	0	333	152	48	0
" 19		1675	241	471	387	0	402	138	36	0
" 26		1478	206	523	115	88	357	147	42	0
August 2		1421	192	437	318	0	328	120	26	0
" 9		1336	180	413	318	0	303	104	18	0
" 16		1309	186	387	331	0	281	116	8	0
" 23		1205	173	307	336	0	294	83	12	0
" 30		1095	164	324	130	148	268	61	0	0
Sept. 6		1319	96	282	257	0	239	40	0	405
" 13		1151	168	255	154	0	178	29	0	369
" 20		873	101	206	340	0	191	35	0	0
" 27		882	83	263	460	0	64	72	0	0
Oct. 4		777	48	241	345	0	143	0	0	0
" 11		760	22	213	468	0	57	0	0	0
" 18		1035	35	178	416	0	38	8	0	360
" 25		815	16	192	558	0	49	0	0	0
Nov. 1		610	9	157	382	0	62	0	0	0
" 8		865	0	106	352	0	47	0	0	360
" 15		527	5	85	382	0	55	0	0	0

DEPT _____

FIGURE 9. A SUMMARY OF IDLENESS CHART

This chart shows how the running time of machines has been increased, due to a knowledge of the causes of idleness. It is a summary of machine charts in one department of a manufacturing plant from July 1 to November 15, on which is copied the total line for the department (see Figure 7). It compares the records for succeeding weeks and emphasizes the progress made toward removing the causes for idleness.

Glancing down the column headed "Lack of Help," it is evident that the idleness due to this cause was considerable and that it was not until September 1 that the foreman was able to make any substantial reduction, but from that time on he made good progress.

Lack of material caused even more idleness than lack of help, and although the situation improved after the first few weeks it was not possible entirely to eliminate idleness due to this cause. The foreman did not have control over the securing of material, for it was bought by the purchasing department, which served the entire plant, and the delays were mostly due to market conditions. A considerable improvement was, however, brought about by closer co-operation between the foreman, the superintendent, and the buyer.

Lack of orders, over which the foreman had no control, became more serious each month and counterbalanced some of the improvement in securing help and material.

Lack of power occurred only twice; repairs were a fertile cause of delay. It is evident, however, that during the last two months charted this matter was well in hand, and although it was impossible to avoid repairs, the time taken to make them was considerably reduced.

From the heavy lines, showing a comparison week by week of the capacity used, it is evident that the running time of the machines of this department was increased in a few months from under 40 to about 70 per cent, in spite of the falling off in orders.

Week Ending June 18, 1921

	PER CENT OF CAPACITY USED (10–90)	TOTAL EXPENSE OF IDLENESS	DETAILS OF IDLENESS EXPENSE DUE TO						
			LACK OF ORDERS	LACK OF HELP	LACK OF TOOLS OR PATTERNS	REPAIRS	LACK OF MATERIAL	WAITING FOR SET-UP	LACK OF CRANE SERVICE
Total Plant		$7588	3277	1413	591	780	1022	57	248
Total Foundry		$4231	1850	934	517	429	253	0	248
Molding Floor #1		166	145	21	0	0	0	0	0
" #2		529	253	66	116	94	0	0	0
" #3		817	155	165	142	107	0	0	248
Large Cores		546	156	42	188	70	90	0	0
Small Cores		675	235	182	63	87	108	0	0
Brass Foundry		774	761	13	0	0	0	0	0
Cleaning Room		724	145	445	8	71	55	0	0
Total Machine Shop		$3157	1427	479	74	351	769	57	
Dept. 1		409	77	99	18	131	27	57	
" 2		561	177	0	3	27	354	0	
" 3		527	300	9	0	0	218	0	
" 4		302	127	0	0	5	170	0	
" 5		1358	746	371	53	188	0	0	

FIGURE 10. A GANTT IDLENESS EXPENSE CHART

This chart shows in actual dollars and cents what it costs to have machines idle. In the plant where it was drawn, the overhead or manufacturing burden was applied to the cost of the product by means of a machine rate. In the foundry, for instance, the cost of owning the land and building and of maintaining the necessary equipment and supervision in order to be ready for work, was distributed to the various molding floors and an hourly rate was arrived at. It is evident that the cost of keeping that floor ready for work went on whether it was used or not and the floor rate was, therefore, charged to idleness accounts according to the reason for that idleness. When work was done on that floor, the wages of the molder and his helpers, if any, together with the cost of material used, were added to this floor rate and charged to the order worked on.

The charts show that the cost of maintaining that part of the total plant which did not do any work and could not, therefore, be charged to any specific manufacturing order amounted to $7,388 for one week. "Lack of orders" caused more idleness than any other single reason, amounting to $3,277. "Lack of help" cost $1,413, and "lack of material" $1,022. In the foundry, "lack of patterns" and "lack of crane service" caused expensive delays. In the machine shop "lack of material" and "lack of help" were serious.

From such a chart as this, the manager of a plant can get an accurate comparison of the ability of his foremen to make use of the equipment under their control and can also fix responsibility for idleness not under the control of foremen.

tion regularly and in detail. In order to get a comprehensive grasp of conditions, he has the records of all his
departments summarized on an Idleness Expense Chart
(Figure 10), showing the cost of idleness of his entire
plant.

Because of his greater experience and broader authority the superintendent can be of most service in
advancing production by helping the foremen overcome
the obstacles with which they are daily confronted and
which they report to him on the Machine Record Chart.

CHAPTER V

THE MAN RECORD CHART

Purpose of Man Record Chart

The purpose of the Man Record Chart is to show whether or not a man does a day's work and, if not, the reason why.

The fact, however, that a man took a certain time to do a piece of work is of but little interest until it is compared with the time in which the work could have been done. The foreman readily sees the advantage of making an estimate of the time it should take before the work is actually begun. If the foreman has accurate information, he makes use of it, but if not, he makes as close an estimate as possible based on his past experience, his estimate approximating the amount of work which any good man should do on a good machine.

As time goes on, the foreman compares the estimated time with the time actually taken and his estimates become more accurate. When he has made use of all the knowledge he has as to the best and quickest way to perform each job, he asks the superintendent for expert assistance in developing still better methods.

Drawing the Man Record Chart

In keeping a Man Record Chart the foreman uses a sheet which is ruled according to the working hours of his shop and is similar to the one used for the Machine Record Chart shown in Figure 7 of the preceding chapter. On the left side of this sheet he lists the men in his control arranged in groups under his subforemen, if he has any. At the top of the sheet he leaves a line for the total of the department.

On the chart the foreman indicates by a line drawn through the daily space how the work done by each man compares with his estimates. The space represents the amount of work the foreman believes should be done; the light line indicates what was done. For instance, an operator has done 150 pieces of work in a day, whereas the foreman believes a good man should do 200. He therefore divides 150 by 200, which gives him 75 per cent, and draws a light line through 75 per cent of the space for that day, thus:

Expressing this in a different way, the space represents the time actually taken to do a certain amount of work, while the light line shows how much time it could reasonably be expected to take. For instance, a workman has taken 8 hours to do work which the foreman had expected him to do in 4 hours. The width of the column for the day represents 8 hours. He therefore draws a light line through an amount of space equal to 4 hours. Another workman has done in 8 hours what the foreman expected would require 12 hours of a good man's time. He therefore draws a light line thus:

through an amount of space equal to 12 hours, i.e., one line all the way across and another halfway across.

Light lines drawn through a second day's space are offset from those of the first day so that they will not appear to be continuations, thus:

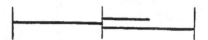

If the foreman has not estimated the time the work should take, he draws a broken line through an amount of space representing the time actually spent on that work, thus:

The portion of the daily space through which no line is drawn shows how much the operator has fallen behind in the work expected of him, and the letter at the beginning of the space indicates the reason, thus:

The reasons which occur most frequently are listed in the key to the Man Record Chart (Figure 11) together with the method of determining which of several reasons should be used. At the end of the week a heavy cumulative line is drawn to show the weekly total of each operator, the heavy line always being equal in length to the sum of the light lines. To get the totals of the various groups and of the whole department, the hours represented by the cumulative lines of the individual workmen are added and divided by the number of men. A line about $\frac{1}{8}$ inch wide is used for a group total and 1/6 inch wide for a department total.

	MAN'S NO.	July MON. 11	TUES. 12	WED. 13	THURS. 14	FRI. 15	SAT. 16	MON. 18	TUES. 19	WED. 20	THURS. 21	FRI. 22	SAT. 23
A. T. White, Foreman													
Kloth, Sub-Foreman													
Schmidt, O.	1	M	M	T						T	R		
Petrusa, J.	17	Y		Y		Y			R		Y		
Braffett, P.	24		G		G	A	A			T			
Feis, Sr.	26	G	G	G	A	A		G	G	R	G	G	G
Schuster, P.	42							R A	Y				
Henderson, H.	31		A	I	I	I		R	I	I	R	I	I
McLaughlin, J.	3						A						
Midenter, Sub-foreman													
Keenan, J.	84	L	L	G	L	L	G	L	T	L	T	L A	L
Volkommer, W.	78	G	G	A	M	G	L	G	R	G	G	G	G
Cerlini, J.	33	M	L	L	I	M	A	L	R	I	R	R	T
MacDowell, A	57	I	I	A	J	I	I	I	L	I	L	T A	L
Mead, T.	43	G	G	G	G	A	G	L	L	L	L	L	L
Haley, R.	36	Y		Y		I	Y						
Brown, W.	21	H	M	M			I	R	A	R	R	L	
Riley, A.	1/4							I	L	I	I	R	
Anderson, P.	18				T			R	R	R	L A	L A	L

FIGURE 11. A GANTT MAN RECORD CHART

LEGEND

— Width of daily space represents amount of work that should have been done in a day.

─── Amount of work actually done in a day.

------- Time taken on work on which no estimate is available.

▮▮▮ Weekly total of operator. Solid line for estimated work; broken line for time spent on work not estimated.

▮▮▮ Weekly total for group of operators.

▮▮▮ Weekly total for department.

The portion of the daily space through which no line is drawn shows how much the man has fallen behind what was expected of him.

REASONS FOR FALLING BEHIND

A—Absent.
G—Green operator.
I—Lack of instructions.
L—Slow operator.
M—Material troubles.
R—Repairs needed.
T—Tool troubles.
V—Holiday.
Y—Smaller lot than estimate is based on.

When there is more than one reason for failure to do the work in estimated time, the reason entered on chart is determined by asking questions in the following order:

R—Was the machine in good condition?
T—Were the tools and fixtures in good condition?
I—Was the operator given proper instructions and sufficient information?
M—Was trouble experienced with material?
G—Was the operator too green to do the job?
L—Was the operator too slow?
Y—Was the lot smaller than estimate is based on?

A change in circumstances may alter the sequence of these questions.

Acting on the Chart

The foreman watches the first line of his chart because it shows him how his department as a whole is living up to his idea of what it should do. If he is not satisfied, he glances over the various group totals to see which group or subforeman has fallen farthest behind. He then looks over the lines for the individuals responsible to that subforeman and studies the detailed reasons why they could not do a full week's work. This enables him to concentrate his attention on the individuals most in need of help and on those hindrances to production which occur most frequently.

The foreman is usually surprised to see that the failure of the operator to do the work within the estimated time is more often his own fault than that of the workman (Figure 12). He learns how much of the time of his men is wasted because of the improper sharpening of tools, defects in materials which should have been caught by the inspectors, the unsatisfactory condition of machines, and the lack of proper instructions on new work. He understands better than ever before why the costs of so many jobs exceed his estimates.

The discovery that possibly nine-tenths of the obstacles which prevent a man from doing a day's work are the fault of the management should not surprise the foreman, for management has assumed the task of securing materials, machines, and tools, of keeping those machines and tools in proper condition for work, of bringing material to the operators when it is needed, of giving workmen complete instructions, and of doing whatever else is necessary to leave the workman free to do the kind of work for which he is best fitted and which gives him the largest return.

Those problems which are the most complicated in modern manufacturing confront the management. The task of the workman, namely, to make use of the knowledge and follow the instructions given him is easier.

The foreman knows that he is judged to a great extent by his ability to run his department so that his men can do a fair day's work and that it is to his advantage to help those who keep the average down. He realizes that the idler and the slow worker require more assistance than the good worker. From the Man Record Charts the foreman secures such information about individual production as enables him to instruct those men who are most in need of help.

Getting the Workman's Co-operation

When he has removed most of the obstacles for which the management is responsible, the foreman shows these charts to his workmen with the idea of developing their ambition and their interest. The charts are so simple that they can be understood by anyone— even by a foreigner who cannot read the language in which they are written. When his line and those of his companions are pointed out to him, he can see how his work compares with that of others.

A foreman soon learns that the long production lines of the two or three men who are head and shoulders above the others seem to have little effect on the average workman, but that the average workman is very strongly influenced by the lines of the men he considers his equals. He hates to be beaten by an equal and

DEPT. E

DEPT. E	MANS NO.	OCT. 19 MON	20 TUES	21 WED	22 THURS	23 FRI	24 SAT	26 MON	27 TUES	28 WED	29 THURS	30 FRI	31 SAT
A.D. Jones, Foreman													
F. Curtis	61												
J. Chryanowsky	109	T	T	T	T	T	T	T		A	A		A
G. Fröhler	235		R	T	R	T	T			R	R	T	
V. Olshewsky	96	T	R	R	R	R		R	R	R	R	R	
J. Kish	79	TR	T	T	T								
O. Shkuda	59	T	T	T	T	T							A
W. Stura	205	T	T	T	T	T							
W. Pagomawiky	93			T	T	T							
L. Olark	38			T	T								
I. Klimbowski	62	T		T	T	T							
F. Harasha	97						G						
P. Fomenko	1	T	T	J	J	T	T						
C. Dorsed	221		R	R	R	R							
S. Szarmach	258		T	T	T	G	T				T	T	
M. Hubok	52	R	R	R	R		R				R	R	R
A. Markofsky	176	T	T				A					A	A
F. Lubas	100	A	A	A	A	A	A	A	A	A	A	A	A
J. Benzerachy	209	A	R			T	T					R	R
O. Cofek	81	HIRED 10/21						LEFT SHOP	A			R	
J. Dubanwitz	150	HIRED 10/21	G	G	GT	6T	G	A	A	G	G	G	G
J. Slivonik	115	HIRED 10/22			T	T	T					T	T
K. Zygo	71							HIRED 10/27 G	G	G	G	GR	R
S. Oroso	272							HIRED 10/27 6	6	6	76	6T	G
J. Novak	281											G	A

42

FIGURE 12. IMPROVEMENT IN CONDITIONS BROUGHT ABOUT BY MAN RECORD CHART

Reasons for falling behind:

   A—Absent or late.
   G—Green operator.
   R—Repairs needed.
   T—Tool troubles or waiting for tools.

This is a copy of the first Man Record Chart made in this department. When it was shown to the plant manager on Friday of the first week, he was surprised to find how much delay in production was caused by tool troubles and machines in need of repairs. He immediately issued instructions to have the tools rigidly inspected and defective ones replaced, and to put a repair gang to work on the machines. He called the foreman and gang bosses into his office, explained the chart to them, and discussed the situation.

The result is shown by the lengthened lines for the following week. The first girl, for instance, J. Curtis, had evidently been so good that in spite of tool troubles during the first week she had fallen only 1 hour short of a week's work, but improved conditions enabled her the second week to do 4 hours more than a week's work. The second girl had trouble with tools, but the second week she increased her output by 4 hours, in spite of the fact that she was absent 4 hours. The third girl had so much trouble with tools and repairs that she did only 4 days' work out of 5½ in the first week, but the attention which the manager gave to the machines and tools enabled her to do 5¼ days' work. The sixth girl during the second week did about 6¾ days' work.

The total lines at the top indicate that the average weekly output had been increased by about 1 day and in a department of 24 girls, this amounted to a considerable increase in production and in earnings for the girls.

The chart also shows that the average production of the department was kept down during the second week by the inexperienced girls recently hired, indicated by G for green operator, and it was made clear that the foreman would have to devote a good deal of his time to their instruction.

will do all he can to keep up with him. But above all he appreciates the opportunity to watch *his own* progress from day to day.

Short-Line Men

There are some workmen, however, who cannot measure up to the average and do not respond to the foreman's effort to stimulate their ambition. These are the men he studies most carefully. Even without records these men know whether they are better or worse than those around them, and they resent the introduction of methods which make this fact evident to the foreman and the other workmen. Those who have in the past tried to cover up their low production by attempting to stand in with the foreman and can no longer do so, are opposed to these records and do all they can to undermine their usefulness.

Experience has taught the foreman that men who feel their inferiority are very apt to do everything possible to distract the attention of others from that fact. This shows itself in flagrant breaches of shop discipline or in creating discontent in the minds of others. In this way they secure an outlet for their energy and distract their own attention, at least, from their inferiority.

When the foreman studies these men who have short lines on the chart, he realizes that this type is usually the backbone of strikes and discord in his department. Their consciousness of inferiority and their discontent is continually smouldering and is easily fanned into flame by some fancied grievance, some real injustice, or some capable agitator. The foreman who wants fewer labor troubles in the future realizes that he must solve the problem of what to do with those men who are below the average—whose lines are short on the chart. Shall he drop them from his pay-roll and ask the employment department to hire others to fill their places? He knows that the available supply of good workmen in most cities, except in times of business depression, is inadequate and that those hired will probably be just as poor as those discharged. If he spends an hour in the employment department watching the applicants, he will see that in good times they are made up largely of men who have never learned to do any job well— men who have been discharged from other jobs because the quality of their work has been poor and their production low.

Discharging the poor workmen in his department will merely add to this mass of floating labor. The foreman who is looking into the future does not discharge these men; he trains them to do at least one job well. He tries them out on various kinds of work until some job is found on which they can do better work than on others. On this job a man is given special instruction, so that no matter how long it takes to bring him up to the average, there are always sufficient instructors to help him. If there is no work in the foreman's own department for which one of these men is fitted, he asks another foreman if he will not try the man out.

This method of handling short-line men appeals to the foreman's sense of fair play, for he is giving these men for once in their lives a real chance to make good. When these men, who formerly had short lines, get to the point where they are turning out a full day's work

DEPT. _____

FOREMAN	WORK DONE COMPARED WITH ESTIMATE	TOTAL HOURS LOST	HOURS LOST DUE TO							
	10 20 30 40 50 60 70 80 90		ABSENCE	GREEN OPERATOR	LACK OF INSTRUCT IDNS	SLOW OPERATOR	MATERIAL TROUBLES	REPAIRS NEEDED	TOOL TROUBLES	SMALL LOT
Week Ending March 26th		716	151	45	146	49	37	278	2	8
April 2		682	155	40	142	48	39	251	3	6
" 9		654	185	40	167	44	35	182	1	0
" 16		596	146	32	130	44	37	175	21	11
" 23		600	131	29	123	26	40	229	8	14
" 30		408	154	16	99	38	25	72	4	0
May 7		473	116	28	113	47	43	120	2	4
" 14		420	132	22	126	42	44	52	0	2
" 21		435	107	18	81	59	44	90	29	7
" 28		286	91	14	69	31	36	44	1	0
June 4		353	113	12	52	36	39	76	19	6
" 11		317	104	10	78	44	42	32	7	0

FIGURE 13. A MAN RECORD SUMMARY CHART

This is a summary of Man Record Charts for a period of 12 weeks. Each line is taken from charts similar to those shown in Figures 11 and 12, and when further information is desired than is given on a summary, it is possible to get full detail from the Man Record Charts.

It is easy to see from this chart that the average production per man in this department was increased from 55 to 80 per cent, and also to see what causes of delay were removed and what were not. Some improvement was made in the matter of absence, but even at the end of the period it amounted to approximately 100 hours per week. The delays due to green operators and lack of instructions were considerably reduced, which made it evident that the foreman was spending a good deal of time in training and developing his employees.

The delays due to slow operators had not been changed to any great extent, that is, the men who were naturally slow on the kind of work assigned to them had not been able to slow much improvement and it had evidently been impossible for the foreman to transfer them to work for which they were better fitted.

Material troubles had continued, but the lost time due to this cause was comparatively small.

Great improvement had been made in reducing the time lost due to the need of repairs to machines and equipment. The figures indicate that for 5 weeks little improvement had become evident, but that after that date conditions were radically changed.

Such a summary chart enables a good foreman to show the results of his work and to get credit for it.

47

week after week, they have almost invariably forgotten their discontent and some of them even show an awakening ambition.

When a man learns to do even one job well, he gets a different outlook on life. A man who for years has considered himself a "wage slave" gains confidence in himself and a control over himself which helps to make a free man of him. He shows possibilities which were entirely unsuspected until he mastered his job.

Long-Line Men

Man Record Charts are invariably welcomed by good workmen, provided the charts are used to help the workmen rather than to drive them. The charts also provide the foreman with a fairly accurate basis for regulating the wages of his operators in accordance with their production. Favoritism and special privilege are done away with and promotions are based on facts rather than impressions.

One day Mr. Gantt in walking through a plant of one of his clients stopped to talk to an operator and asked him what he thought of the Man Record Charts. The operator replied, "I always knew I was the best man in the shop, but no one would believe it. Now everyone knows it." For the first time in his experience this man had secured proper credit for the work he did and it was natural for him to welcome these records.

The workman who thinks, knows that he cannot continue indefinitely to get paid for a good day's work when he does only half a day's work and he resents the continued recurrence of difficulties which will not enable him to do a full day's work. When he brought these delays to the attention of the foreman, he was often considered a "kicker"; but when the obstacles are brought to the foreman's attention by means of charts, an unusual degree of co-operation is secured between the foreman and the workman. Careful consideration is given by the foreman to a workman's suggestions for improvements which will increase his output, because to do so is to the foreman's interest, since an increase in output will lengthen his production line as well as the operator's.

The workman sees the man whose line is longest, whose production is greatest, appointed to the position of subforeman when there is a vacancy. He sees the subforeman whose group line is longest become a foreman. As he watches these changes take place throughout the organization and positions of authority given to men who "know what to do and how to do it," he sees opening up before him possibilities of advancement limited only by his ability and his interest.

The Superintendent

In order to get the help of the superintendent in removing delays over which he himself has no control, the foreman sends copies of his Man Record Charts to the superintendent each week. With them he sends a Man Record Summary (Figure 13) showing the total line of the department for each week. This summary enables the superintendent to see very clearly any tendencies toward lower production and to take whatever steps may be necessary to guide his shop policy. It also enables him to reward his workmen according to the amount of work done (Figure 14).

4

SUMMARY FOR SHARING PROFITS

DEPT. F.	GIRL'S NO.	NOVEMBER 1921					DECEMBER					
		12	19	26	3	10	17	24	31			
TOTAL DEPARTMENT												
Burt, F.	142											
Consler, D.	368											
Dow, G.	206											
Evans, A.	590											
Jones, H.	154											
Lovejoy, M.	78											
Moore, M.	342											
Moore, R.	362											
Palmer, H.	374											
Price, N.	344											
Schaeffer, B.	382											
Sondel, P.	371											
Smith, J.	359											

50

FIGURE 14. MAN RECORD SUMMARY USED FOR SHARING PROFITS

In the shop where this chart was drawn, the company shared its profits with its employees. These profits were figured for each 8 weeks' period and apportioned to the various departments of the business according to the way they measured up to the standard of performance agreed upon. This was done by means of a chart similar to the above, except that it showed departments instead of individual operators.

When the amount of profit was apportioned to a department, it was distributed to the individuals in that department on the basis shown in the above chart. The light lines for the various weeks on this chart were taken from weekly Man Record Charts (Figures 11 and 12). With this plan the girls were convinced of the fairness of distribution of the profits within their depart-

ment because they could figure it out for themselves. This chart showed the output of each girl for the 8 weeks' period and for each individual week. If there was any question as to the accuracy of this summary the operator could refer to the Man Record Charts for the various weeks which showed the reasons for not doing a day's work. It was possible to go even farther back and consult the "man record cards" on which were listed daily the jobs done by each girl with the estimated time and the actual time taken on each job.

The distribution of profits by this method was fair because it was based on the actual production of each operator with no guesses and no chance for favoritism. The method was so clear that the operator could understand every step taken.

When the estimates of all the departments are made on the same basis, the superintendent is also enabled to compare the ability of his various foremen to get work done. Since production is the aim of the entire organization and these charts point out the men who are successful in getting production, the superintendent or the manager will be able to build up an organization composed of men who have proved their ability to produce.

CHAPTER VI

THE LAYOUT CHART

Use of Layout Chart in Planning

Idleness of men and machines is usually the greatest source of waste in a manufacturing plant, and yet it is possible to take definite steps to prevent its recurrence by presenting to the management in such detail as to fix responsibility, the reasons for idleness, such as lack of help, material, orders, tools, etc. This is done by planning work sufficiently far in advance to advise each individual concerned what he is to do and when. In some plants where a uniform product is manufactured this is not a difficult matter. If, for instance, 100 machines are being made each week, every foreman or workman knows that he is to turn out enough parts to make 100 machines. The planning in such a case is very simple and can sometimes be done without any written record.

There are very few plants, however, which produce only one article—usually a department has to turn out a great many different parts to be used in the assembling of a varied product. Moreover, it is probable that these different parts are worked on in other departments also. It therefore becomes necessary for the foreman to plan carefully the work to be done on each machine in his department and also for the superintendent or manager to plan the work to be done in all the departments of the plant.

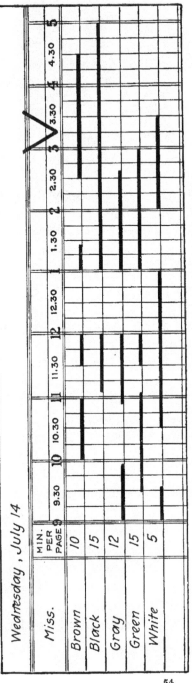

FIGURE 15. LAYOUT IN A STENOGRAPHIC DEPARTMENT

This sheet is ruled in accordance with the working hours of the department, that is, from 9 to 5, and on account of the nature of the work the hours are divided into 15-minute periods.

At 9 o'clock the lines indicate that Miss Gray and Miss White were the only ones who had work left over from the previous day. At 9:30 Miss Green returned from taking dictation with notes in her book which would take about an hour and a half to transcribe.

When this chart was reproduced at 3:15 P.M., the first two stenographers had work ahead of them, the next two had nothing ahead and could take more dictation.

This chart is a valuable aid in getting letters out the day they are dictated.

54

The Gantt Layout Chart is used in working out a plan to get the orders in hand done when they are wanted and to make the best possible use of the available men and machines. No method of doing this can be satisfactory unless it emphasizes above everything else when jobs are to be begun, by whom, and how long they will take.

In a Stenographic Department

One of the simplest forms of the Gantt Layout Chart is that used in assigning work to stenographers. With the two ends in view of sending stenographers to the same dictators whenever possible and of getting all work out the day it is dictated, the proper assignment of stenographers becomes a difficult problem. It is necessary for the head stenographer to know at all times how much work each operator has ahead of her, so that when she receives a call for stenographic service she will not have to take the time to ask the individual operators how soon they will finish the work in hand.

The head stenographer takes a sheet ruled to show the hours of the day and divides the hour either into six columns representing 10 minutes each or four columns representing 15 minutes (Figure 15). On the left side of the sheet she lists the stenographers and shows the time it takes each individual to write out one page of her notes. This figure does not represent the best possible time but the time the operator takes normally.

When a stenographer comes back to the stenographic department after taking dictation, she lays on the head stenographer's desk a slip of paper showing the time of her return and the number of pages of notes to be transcribed. The head stenographer multiplies the number of pages by the minutes per page which appear on the layout sheet. This will give her the time it will take for that individual to complete the work in her book. The head stenographer draws a line on the layout sheet representing this amount of time, beginning at the time noted on the slip of paper which the stenographer has placed on her desk. When this has been done for all the operators in the department, the head stenographer can see at a glance from her layout sheet when each stenographer will complete her work.

When a dictator calls for a stenographer, she looks to see if the one who is in the habit of handling that man's work can take this dictation and get it out that day. If not, the head stenographer sends to the dictator the one who will first be available.

One of the most difficult problems in handling a stenographic department is to get all the letters into the mail the day they are dictated. To get these letters out, it is necessary to distribute them evenly over the available stenographers so that one will not be loaded up with two days' work while another sits waiting.

If the capacity of the whole stenographic department is taken up for the day and a dictator calls for a stenographer, the head stenographer will then tell him that it is impossible to get out any more work that day unless he prefers to have left over until the next day some of the letters he has already dictated.

Another advantage of this plan is that the work is evenly assigned to stenographers, so that if the work is light they all finish early in the afternoon and if it is heavy, they all work up to closing time.

In a Machine Shop

The planning of work in a machine shop is more complicated and the Layout Chart must show more detail in regard to the work to be done (Figure 16).

A sheet is used which is ruled to represent the working hours of the plant, the ruling depending upon the average length of jobs. If they extend over several weeks, the wide columns represent weeks and the narrow ones days; if they run less than a week, the wide columns represent days and the narrow ones hours; if they last less than a day, the wide columns represent hours and the narrow ones fractions of hours.

All the machines or work-benches in a department or shop are listed on the left side of this sheet. When an order is received, a list of the operations through which the material is to go is looked up, if it is not already shown on the order. On the Layout Chart opposite the machine to be used, the first operation is laid out.

An angle opening to the right:

⌐

indicates when the job is to be started.

An angle opening to the left:

⌐

indicates when the job is scheduled to be completed.

A light line connecting the angles indicates the total time scheduled for the order:

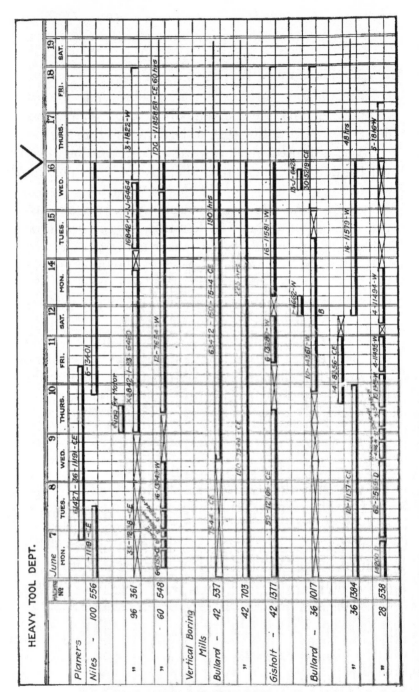

FIGURE 16. A GANTT LAYOUT CHART FOR A MACHINE SHOP

LEGEND

⌐ Date job is scheduled to start.

¬ Date job is scheduled to be completed.

[Total time scheduled for order.

▮ Work done.

▨ Time required to make up for past delays.

Figures above lines indicate order numbers.

> Indicates that chart was reproduced Wednesday night and shows how the work stood at that time.

REASONS FOR STOPPING WORK

B—Break-up.
H—Lack of help.
M—Lack of material.
P—Lack of power.
R—Repairs.
T—Lack of tools.

This layout chart was drawn in a department equipped with large machine tools. On such machines only one job can be done at a time. On the first machine part

No. 11191-CE, according to the foreman's estimate, was to have been finished Tuesday noon, but had been completed on Monday and another order was begun, No. 61427. That job was also finished ahead of estimate and the third order was begun Thursday afternoon instead of Friday. When the chart was copied on Wednesday, the 16th, the work was just on schedule.

On the second machine, the work was already 3 days behind schedule when it was carried over from a previous sheet. At that time, order X6842 was scheduled to be begun Thursday morning and completed Monday afternoon, but it was necessary to run in a repair job, a ring for a motor, so that 4 hours had to be allowed for the delay (indicated by crossed lines) before No. 16842 could be begun. When the chart was copied; Wednesday night, the work on this machine was 4 hours behind schedule.

The machine on which the next operation is to be
done is looked up on the chart to see when it will be
ready for additional work. The order is then assigned
to this machine and the angles and the light line are
drawn. This procedure is followed in laying out all
the operations on that order and continued until all
the orders are laid out.

In assigning work to machines it is necessary to
know what progress has been made on the work already
assigned. Accordingly, as daily reports are received
showing the amount of work done, a heavy line is drawn
under the light line:

If the work is exactly on schedule, the end of the
heavy line will be directly under the proper date and
hour. If the work is behind or ahead of schedule, the
end of the heavy line will be behind or ahead of the
date. In assigning a new order to a machine, if the
work is *ahead of schedule,* the new order is placed over

MON.	TUES.	WED.	THURS.	FRI.
			A424	
A423				

FIGURE 17. HOW WORK AHEAD OF SCHEDULE IS SHOWN
BY THE GANTT LAYOUT CHART

the old one (Figure 17) and the date of beginning is
placed in advance of the date of completion of the old
order.

The V indicates the date on which the chart is copied. The work is 1 day ahead of schedule and conditions in the shop indicate that it will be 1 day early in finishing. The new order, A424, is therefore laid out to be begun Thursday morning.

If the work is *behind schedule*, there is no advantage in planning to begin the new order until the old one is complete. Therefore sufficient time must be set aside to make up for past delays before the new work can be begun. This is done by connecting the angles by crossed lines (Figure 18).

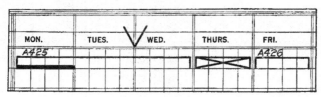

FIGURE 18.   HOW WORK BEHIND SCHEDULE IS SHOWN BY
THE GANTT LAYOUT CHART

On the date indicated by the V the work was 1 day behind schedule. Before assigning order A426, 1 day is allowed to make up for the delay and is indicated by crossed lines.

Above the light lines are written whatever numbers and quantities may be necessary to identify the orders.

When work stops on any order a jog is placed under the line with an initial to indicate the reason.

The usual reasons are repairs, lack of help, material, power, or tools, as shown by the legend accompanying Figure 16.

MOLDERS	FLOOR Nº	24 MON	25 TUE	26 WED	27 THURS.	28 FRI	29 SAT.	31 MON	1 TUE	2 WED	3 THURS.	4 FRI	5 SAT.

909 Conden — 57
5-44-12+ 66-7 W-Pedestal
341-5-13880 Cyl 1 Per Day
286-3-13042 W- Cylinder
B
5-424-8 8640 W-Pistan 1 Per Day
5024-21-1464 W- Pedestal
5602-3-13515-W
B 5482-7-8691 W-Piston-2 Per Day
H
H

901 Kelsey — 58
5493-30-8645 CE Plate
170-50-8646 CE Plate

866 Malone — 58-2
538-8-13-78 SW
204-4-13210 W-Head
7263-25-12983 W-Heads
282-2-1319 W-Piston
1331F
6744-20-12767 W-4 Per Day R
2713280R
261-24-13463 W 18 1 Per Day
285-6-13273 W-Head
13283-Replace 11424 W-Replace
Piston Nº 6

965 Piper — 59
5705-30-834 W-To-Do
3570 W-Hose-1 Per Day
5420-12-8476 W-Crosshead-1 Per Day
5416-40 W-Hose-2 Per Day
5280-B-4014
8-4-9-Replace

859 Richardson — 59-2
541-10-13-393 W-Cover 1 Per Day
5505-12-8356 W-Gear-2 Per Day
6263-12-8056 W-Gear 1 Per Day
5477-12 8636 W
6646-
6646 W
1426 W
011-6-13715 W-Arm-2 Per Day
6432
1-11339 W-Threaded
5430-8-4804
453-2-3814 W
452-4-6363 W
451-4-6364 W
6581-3288 W-4

Figure 19. A Gantt Layout Chart for a Foundry

On the molding floors in a foundry it is possible to do more than one order at a time. This makes the laying out of work different from that for machine tools, as shown in Figure 16.

On this chart the first molder, Conden, on floor No. 57, could put up molds for three orders each day. The chart indicates that he worked on order No. 5144 until Wednesday morning, when he was instructed to "break up" (indicated by B) and start on order No. 286. When he finished that he began on No. 341, but had to be stopped on account of lack of help (H) Tuesday morning, the 1st, when he went back to the first order No. 5144 and did a day's work.

The second order, No. 5428, on which he was working on Monday, the 24th, went ahead until Friday morning, when he had to break up and began order No. 5462, on which he worked until Monday morning when the absence of his helper prevented him from continuing.

On his third order, No. 5228, after 1 day's work he broke up and worked on order No. 300.

When the chart was copied Tuesday night, the 1st, Conden was so far behind the work already assigned to him that crossed lines had to be drawn through the remainder of the week to indicate that that amount of time would be required to make up for past delays before any further orders could be assigned to him.

63

This graphic layout makes it possible to group orders and distribute them over the available machines in a much more intelligent manner than by the hit-or-miss method of deciding what the next job will be whenever a machine runs out of work. When a machine breaks down, it is easy to transfer work from it to other machines without disturbing the proper sequence of work. When it is desirable to rush a certain order through ahead of other work, the use of a layout chart makes it possible to do so with maximum speed because the chart visualizes not only the time required to do the rush order but to get the other work out of its way. There is an added advantage in that the chart shows clearly how this rush order interfers with the work already in the plant and makes it possible to revise any promises which are likely to be broken.

Other Plants

In a machine shop or textile plant work is planned by machines (Figure 16), but in a foundry by floors, benches, or machines (Figure 19). The chart for the heavy tool department (Figure 16) illustrates the planning of work for machine tools on which only one job can be done at one time. On drills with more than one spindle, on grinders with two wheels, and other machines, it is possible to run more than one job at a time. On a molding floor in a foundry, for instance, the molder frequently works on several jobs in a day, the number depending on the importance of the work, the number of patterns he has for each order, the time necessary to put up each mold, and the size of the floor.

In a Foundry

The Layout Chart for a foundry (Figure 19) shows how a variety of orders is planned for each man. Molder No. 909, Conden, is behind schedule, which is indicated by the fact that the heavy lines representing work done do not run to Tuesday night when the chart was reproduced, as shown by the *V*. The reason he is behind is made clear by the *B's* showing that he had had to break up on some orders and start new ones, and by the *H's,* which indicate that his helper was absent for a day. The last molder on the sheet, No. 859, Richardson, is ahead of schedule on all but one of his orders.

It will be observed that the heavy lines on the Gantt Layout Chart show how much work has been done and how far it is behind or ahead of the schedule, but they do not show just when the work was done. If an attempt were made to show that information also, the chart would become so complicated that it would not be clear. The purpose of the Layout Chart is to plan work; it is necessary to show how the work stands when a new job is assigned, but it is not necessary to know in detail what has happened in the past. That can be done much more effectively on a Gantt Progress Chart.

The same type of Layout Chart is used by the various foremen and by the central planning office, except that the foremen plan only one day in advance while the planning office lays out all the work ahead of the plant.

The Gantt Layout Chart is much more satisfactory than a layout board because it is more easily handled. It does not require any wall space, but can be used on

5

a desk or table, kept in a drawer, and carried around easily. Work is laid out in pencil and no expensive equipment is needed.

It is never necessary to erase anything from a Layout Chart unless a mistake has been made. If work has been laid out according to the best knowledge available at the time and further information obtained at a later date makes a change advisable, the original plan is allowed to remain on the sheets and "Transferred to ...." is written over it. This makes clear all the steps taken and the reasons for changes in plans.

The Gantt Layout Chart helps to get work done because it makes clear who is to do any piece of work, when it is to be done, and how long it will take. It can be successfully made out only by one who knows what is to be done, how it can be done, and how long it will take. Instructions based on this chart will, therefore, create confidence in the mind of the one who is to do the work. It is possible through this chart to assign definite tasks, and the more definite the task the easier it is to get it done.

CHAPTER VII

THE LOAD CHART

Difference Between Layout Chart and Load Chart

The purpose of the Gantt Load Chart is to keep the executives of any producing plant advised as to the load of work ahead of their plant. This information is of particular value to managers, superintendents, foremen, employment departments, and sales departments, for it gives them an accurate picture of the work which is to be done and it is necessary to have a clear understanding of that before effective steps can be taken to do it.

The Load Chart is similar to the Layout Chart in that it shows how much work is to be done, but it is more compact than the Layout Chart and does not show details. Layout Charts show each operation on each order and the individual machines which are to do the work, but a Load Chart merely shows classes of machines and the hours of work assigned to them by weeks or months. The drawing of the Load Chart is similar to that of the Progress Chart so far as light and heavy lines are concerned; but the similarity ends there, for the Progress Chart shows work done and lines are added as more work is done; but the Load Chart shows only work which is *to be done* and represents the status of plans at a specified date. It is not a record added to day by day but an analysis of a situation at a given moment.

How the Gantt Load Chart Is Drawn

At the left of the sheet are listed the classes or groups of operators, machines, work-benches, or floors and in the next column the numbers in each group. In the columns representing months or weeks, the figures indicate the number of operating hours for a group of men or machines; the light lines show the hours of work which have been assigned to that group during each week or month; and the cumulative lines represent the total hours of work ahead of each group. The information for this chart is secured from Layout Charts which show what orders are ahead of each machine, and from this it is easy to foot up the hours of work planned for the various classes of machines for each week or month.

When a picture of the amount of work ahead of a plant is placed before an executive on a Load Chart, it is possible for him so to grasp the situation that he can adjust equipment, operators, and working hours to the amount of work ahead or adapt the work to the equipment and operators.

If there is *a great amount of work* ahead, he can secure information from the Load Chart as to:

1. What deliveries may be quoted on future orders.
2. What kinds of orders must be declined.
3. Where congestion is likely to occur, so that those processes can be studied, shortened, or improved.
4. What additional equipment to buy.
5. How many men to employ and the kind of work they will have to do.
6. Where hours need to be lengthened.

If there is *not enough work* ahead, the manager can learn from the chart:

1. What kinds of orders are needed to keep the men or equipment busy (this information may be the basis of sales or advertising campaigns, of reductions in prices, etc.).
2. What men to assign to other work.
3. What equipment can be disposed of.
4. Where hours should be shortened.

In order to furnish this information a Load Chart must be accurate and up to date, but this is not difficult if the Load Chart is based on Layout Charts such as were described in the preceding chapter.

A Foundry Load Chart

In the foundry where the Load Chart illustrated in Figure 20 was drawn the main divisions of the work were iron, steel, brass, and core-making; and in the iron foundry, for instance, the secondary divisions were "crane floors," "side floors," "bench floors," and "squeezer machines." The molds for the largest castings were put up on the crane floors because they were served by large cranes. On the side floors they poured medium-sized castings which could be lifted by jib cranes or by hand, and on the bench floors and squeezer machines they made the smallest sizes.

When this particular chart was placed on the superintendent's desk, he saw that on the crane floors of the iron foundry there were 16 molders whose hours per week amounted to 640. For the first week charted, 310 hours of work had been assigned to them, which

	NO. OF MOLDERS		Sept.	October	November	December

	NO.OF MOLDERS	
Total Foundry	92	3680
Iron Foundry	48	1920
Crane Floors	16	640
Side Floors	20	800
Bench Floors	10	400
Squeezer Mach.	2	80
Steel Foundry	12	480
Crane Floors	2	80
Side Floors	4	160
Bench Floors	4	160
Squeezer Mach	2	80
Brass Foundry	6	240
Side Floors	0	
Bench Floors	2	80
Squeezer Mach.	4	160
Core Making	26	1040
Large Cores	14	560
Small Cores	12	480

Months: Sept. 24 | Oct. 1, 8, 15, 22, 29 | Nov. 6, 13, 20, 27 | Dec. 3, 10

FIGURE 20. A GANTT LOAD CHART USED IN A FOUNDRY

This chart indicated how the work ahead of the foundry stood on Monday, September 19. In the iron foundry there were 16 molders on the crane floors, and since the foundry was running 40 hours per week, the molding hours of these men per week amounted to 640. That amount was, therefore, used as a scale for each week. These molders were at that time behind schedule on about 320 hours of work, which was represented by a heavy broken line through half of the first week. For that week there was scheduled on the Layout Charts, similar to that shown in Figure 19, a little more than half a week's work. This was represented by a light line. For several succeeding weeks, the work scheduled amounted to less than half of the capacity of these molders. The heavy line indicated the total time required to do the work assigned to them, that is, that it would have taken about 2½ weeks to do all the work, if the men could have worked steadily at it.

The side floors had more molders and enough work to keep them busy several weeks longer. The total capacity of the iron foundry, as indicated by the wider line, was taken up for 3½ weeks.

The steel foundry, however, had a great deal more work ahead than could be done by the molders assigned to that foundry. On the side floors, for instance, they were already about 3 weeks behind schedule, as indicated by the broken line, and for several weeks more work was scheduled than could be done by that number of molders. There was a similar condition on the bench floors and the chart made it clear that unless more men were assigned to the steel foundry, the work would not be completed until December 3, although the last promise of delivery, indicated by light lines, was the week of November 6.

This chart emphasized the unbalanced condition of work in this foundry and the need for shifting workmen in such a way that all promises of delivery could be met.

Shop No. 10. Load on Machine Tools.

	NO. OF MACH.	OCT.	NOV.	DEC.	JAN.	FEB.	MCH.
H.B. Mill for Casings	1						Z
Blade Millers	12						Z
Vert. B. Mills	11						Z
Drill Presses	4						Z
Milling Machines	2						Z
Lucas B Mills	1					Z	
H.B. Mills	1	Z	Z			Z	
Lathes	6					Z	
Lathes for Shafts	1	Z			Z		
Blade Grinders	3						Z
Grinders	1	Z	Z	Z	Z		

Note: Above Chart is based on Number of Operators now Employed.

	NO. OF MACH.	OCT.	NOV.	DEC.	JAN.	FEB.	MCH.
H.B. Mills for Casings	1						Z
Blade Millers	31				Z		
Vert B. Mills	20					Z	
Drill Presses	9						Z
Milling Machines	8					Z	
Lucas B. Mills	2			Z		Z	
H.B. Mills	3	Z	Z		Z	Z	
Lathes	23					Z	
Lathes for Shafts	2				Z		
Blade Grinders	6				Z		
Grinders	2	Z	Z	Z	Z		

Note: Above Chart is based on 100% Running Capacity

FIGURE 21. A GANTT LOAD CHART USED IN A MACHINE SHOP

This chart shows how far in the future the machine tools will be kept busy by orders in the plant when it is drawn up. On the first line, for instance, it is clear that the one horizontal boring mill will be busy 80 per cent of the time during October, 20 per cent during November, and all of December and January. The heavy lines indicate that the work ahead of these machines is not well balanced.

This chart was drawn at a time when the machine shop did not have a normal amount of work. Some of the operators were laid off and their machines shut down, and therefore in the upper half of the illustration the work ahead of this reduced force was charted. To prevent anyone from getting the impression that this chart represented the capacity of the plant, the same amount of work was also charted against the total capacity of the machines.

would keep them busy half their time. For the 5 succeeding weeks 30 per cent or less of their time would be required. The cumulative line showed him that half a week's work was behind the schedule for lack of patterns and other reasons, and that the total work ahead amounted to the molders' capacity for only 2½ weeks, although that work would have to be spread over 6 weeks.

In the steel foundry, however, the superintendent saw that there was more work to be done on the side and bench floors than could be done by the molders assigned to those floors. In all there was 12 weeks' work ahead and it was wanted in 7 weeks. It was important to deliver the castings when they were wanted, so the superintendent immediately issued instructions to run an additional heat each day and he transferred 2 molders from the brass to the steel foundry. He knew that these changes would enable him to make the deliveries promised. In the iron and brass foundries there was not enough work to keep the molders busy, so the superintendent reduced the hours per week until additional orders could be secured.

This Load Chart enabled the superintendent to reduce the idleness in his plant, but, above all, to deliver the castings when they were wanted.

A Load Chart for Machine Tools

The Gantt Load Chart shows very clearly whether or not the machine tools in a plant are going to be kept busy in the near future—which ones are overloaded and which have little work ahead. In Figure 21 the machine tools in shop No. 10 are listed in groups and the

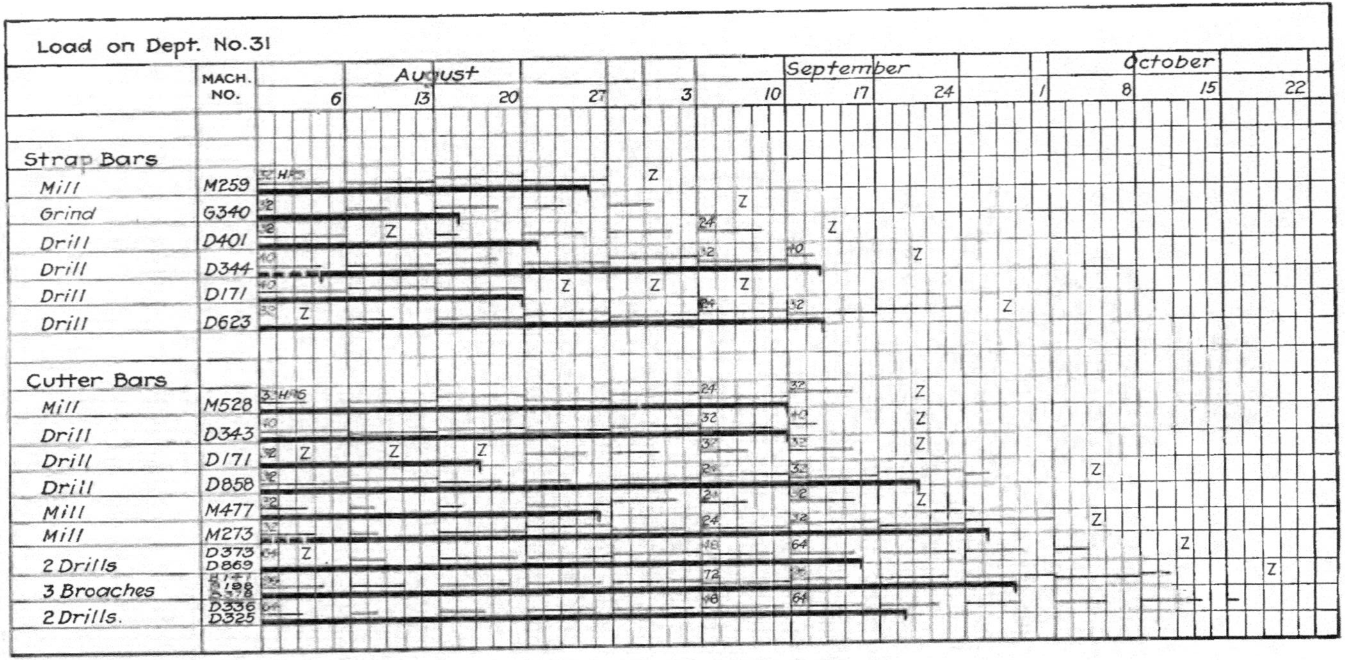
Load on Dept. No.31
MACH. NO.
August
September
October
6
13
20
27
3
10
17
24
1
8
15
22
Strap Bars
Mill
M259
Grind
G340
Drill
D401
Drill
D344
Drill
D171
Drill
D623
Cutter Bars
Mill
M528
Drill
D343
Drill
D171
Drill
D858
Mill
M477
Mill
M273
2 Drills
D373
D869
3 Broaches
2 Drills.
D336
D325

FIGURE 22. A GANTT LOAD CHART FOR A MACHINE SHOP DEPARTMENT

This chart shows the amount of work planned for each machine or group of machines in a department which worked on two kinds of parts, strap and cutter bars. On the first machine, M259, which ran 32 hours per week, work was assigned for the week ending the 6th which would keep the machine running only 80 per cent of the time. For the 3 weeks following, its capacity was taken up, but after that there was no work ahead.

The second machine, G340, had no work assigned for the first week and about half of its capacity taken up for the next 4 weeks.

The fifth machine, D191, was running 40 hours a week and its capacity was covered by assignments for the first 3 weeks. At that time the fixtures were to be changed on the machine so that it could work on cutter bars, so it reappeared on the chart as the 3rd machine in the 2nd group and for 4 weeks its capacity was a little more than half taken up. While engaged on that work, it was operated on a 32-hour week.

This chart gave the superintendent a clear understanding of the amount of work ahead of this department, so that he could arrange the number of men needed to operate the machines and the number of hours each week that machines should be run. The chart emphasized the fact that some of the operations were not well balanced, that is, that some of the machines, particularly in the first group, turned out their work twice as fast as other machines. By concentrating attention on the advisability of shortening the processes on some of these machines, better fixtures were designed.

lines show what part of the time they will be kept running to turn out the orders then in hand. This chart was drawn in a period of dull business and the information was, therefore, presented in two ways, the first half of the chart listing only those machines to which operators were assigned at that time, and the second half listing all the machines in the shop. The latter half, therefore, shows well in advance what machine tools will be idle unless more orders are secured, while the first half goes further and, in addition to telling what machines will be idle, shows what operators will have to be kept in the shop in idleness or be laid off if no more work is provided.

In this plant it was not necessary for the superintendent to spend hours in conversation with his foremen in an attempt to learn just how much work they had ahead of them, nor did he have to read long reports; on the Load Chart he had accurate information in condensed form.

A Load Chart for a Department

In issuing orders for manufacture, it is desirable to know what work is already in the plant and when the machines will be free for additional orders. Figure 22 shows the machines in a shop department listed according to the sequence of operations. For instance, the first operation on a strap bar was milling and it was done on machine M259; the next was grinding on machine G340; etc. The lines show that the orders then in the department would keep the first machine busy for only 4 weeks; the second machine, G340, would have no work during the first week and about half a week's work for each of the next 4 weeks; the third machine, D401, would be busy the whole of the first week, but have nothing to do the second week.

The chart emphasizes the fact that the operations were not well balanced, i.e., it took so long for some machines to do their part of the work that those on succeeding operations would have to stand idle a part of the time. For instance, the first machine, although it ran all the time for 4 weeks, would keep the second and third busy only part of each week. The chart made it clear that the first operation should be speeded up by some means in order to manufacture these parts economically, and an investigation revealed that improved jigs and fixtures were needed.

As to the cutter bars, the chart made it clear that the orders then in the department could not be completed on the last operation for about 11 weeks, and that the breakdown of a machine or the absence of an operator would have a serious effect on the output of the department.

In a drop forge plant it is necessary to promise delivery on each order and that delivery depends largely on the work already assigned to the hammers. A Load Chart (Figure 23) shows how far the capacity of the hammers is taken up by orders already entered.

The amount of work ahead of any manufacturing plant constantly varies and the management must be able to change its plans as quickly as the work changes. Whatever action is taken, must be based on accurate information as to the status at that particular time—never

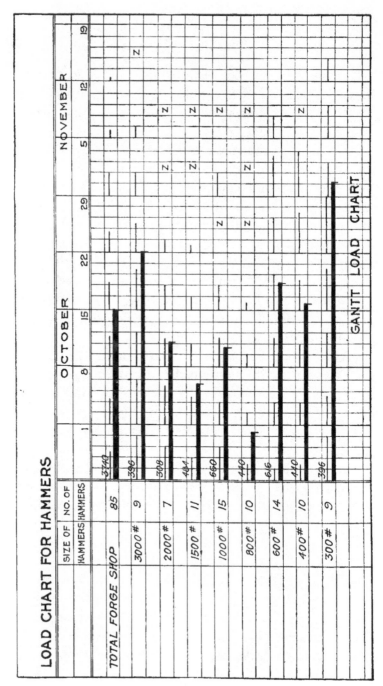

LOAD CHART FOR HAMMERS

GANTT LOAD CHART

FIGURE 23. LOAD CHART FOR A DROP FORGE PLANT

On this chart the total amount of work ahead of the hammers was shown according to the time it would take to do it.

The second line of the chart showed that there were nine 3,000-pound hammers in the shop operating 44 hours in a week and that, therefore, the capacity of the group was 396 hours. The work assigned to them during the first week would keep them busy 80 per cent of the time, as was shown by the light line. The same amount of work was booked for the second week, but for the week ending November 12 only 20 per cent of their capacity was taken up. The heavy line showed that the total work ahead of the 3,000-pound hammers would keep them busy to capacity for 4 weeks if it were possible to go straight ahead without waiting for dies and steel.

The amount of work ahead of the various groups of hammers varied considerably, the 800-pound hammers having less than a week's work and the 300-pound group more than 5 weeks.

The first line on the chart showed the work ahead of the forge shop as a whole. For the first week the light line showed that 50 per cent of the capacity was taken up, but the percentage gradually decreased until only 10 per cent was taken up in the week of November 19.

The first heavy line indicates that the orders ahead of the total forge shop would equal its capacity for 3 weeks, if those orders could be spread evenly over the hammers of all sizes.

This chart was used as the basis for quoting prices. When there was not much work ahead of a certain class of hammers, low prices would be quoted in order to secure more orders; with a good deal of work ahead of hammers of a given size, high prices would be quoted in order to secure only the most desirable orders.

on general impressions which have been carried over from some previous time.

The Gantt Load Chart gives the manager or super-intendent an insight into the future which it is very nearly impossible for him to get in any other way.

CHAPTER VIII

THE PROGRESS CHART

Purpose of the Progress Chart

The purpose of the Gantt Progress Chart is to show what progress is being made in the execution of a plan or program.

One of the fundamental principles of management was formulated by Gantt when he said: *"The authority to issue an order involves the responsibility to see that it is executed."* It is obvious, therefore, that when an executive, i.e., anyone who has control over others, has issued instructions that certain things are to be done, his next step is to provide a mechanism which will at all times keep him advised as to whether or not his orders are being carried out and, if the progress is not satisfactory, will tell him the reason why. The Gantt Progress Chart gives this information clearly and concisely and, since the facts are presented in their relation to time, the chart induces action.

Some executives look back over their records at the end of a given period of time, possibly a year or a month, compare actual accomplishment with what they believed was possible, and conclude that the performance was either good or bad. It is the wise executive, however, who goes carefully over conditions at the beginning of any period, studies the tendencies, and decides then what performance will be satisfactory. This is his plan or schedule. Should there be, later on,

6   81

a marked change in conditions which it was not possible for him to foresee, he will, of course, make the necessary alterations in the schedule.

In this way the executive relieves himself of the necessity of analyzing records every time a new figure is received, comparing it with other figures and deciding whether it is good or bad. Usually in the rush of business, comparison of this kind is likely to be done hastily, and the decision is apt to be unwise. However, where the executive determines beforehand what will be satisfactory to him, he is almost sure to study the matter thoroughly and to secure all the expert advice and accurate information available.

After this schedule is worked out, a comparison of accomplishment with the plan becomes merely a clerical task; the executive's time is saved and he is left free to study the tendencies and take the action indicated by the records.

The Value of the Gantt Progress Chart

In this phase of an executive's work the Gantt Progress Chart is of inestimable value. Its use makes a definite plan necessary and presents that plan so clearly that it can be readily understood in detail and as a whole by the executive's associates and subordinates. It compares the performance with the plan both as to time and amounts, and makes it possible for the executive to foresee future happenings with considerable accuracy. It shows what part of the work has been done in accordance with the schedule and emphasizes the reasons why performance has fallen short of the plan, fixing responsibility for its success or failure.

Usually it is not necessary for the higher executive to follow on Progress Charts all the details of the work being done under his direction, but he does wish to follow the progress of the work as a whole, which may be done by following key operations, typical items, or totals. If the progress made on one of these subdivisions of the work is satisfactory, he will pay little attention to it, but if another part of the work is behind schedule, he will call for the detail charts in the hands of one of his subordinates. From these records he can see what particular items are being delayed and the reasons. He can then concentrate his efforts on that particular problem and, because of his broader authority and greater resourcefulness, may overcome difficulties which to his subordinates are insurmountable.

Saving Time for the Executive

This method makes it unnecessary for the general manager of a manufacturing plant, for instance, to wade through volumes of reports or to go the rounds of his superintendents or foremen in an attempt to find out what work is not progressing satisfactorily. His subordinates are likely to minimize the importance of some delays and on other items not to realize the effect a short delay will have on other work. Gantt charts emphasize the fact that time is the most important element in production—they bring to the attention of the general manager the things which are most urgent and hold his attention until he takes action and sees the results.

The Progress Chart also enables the general manager to know whether or not he will be able to live up to whatever promises of delivery he has made, for he knows that a reputation for keeping promises is one of the most valuable assets of any organization. Of course, the ability to make quick deliveries will frequently secure an order which would otherwise be lost, but quick deliveries depend entirely on the volume of work ahead. If a customer is continually promised quick deliveries by a certain plant and much later deliveries by its competitors, the reputation of that plant will be injured rather than enhanced, for the customer is likely to conclude either that the poor quality of the product prevents the plant from securing orders or that another customer's orders are being set aside for his. One impression is as detrimental as the other, for the customer knows that if another customer's work is set aside for his, it is probable that his work will be set aside for the next insistent customer.

It is clear, therefore, that a reputation for deliveries must be founded on the ability to live up to whatever promises are made. If a promise of delivery is to be kept, all the work in a plant must be planned so accurately that, when a new order is received, it is possible to tell almost to a day when the work will be completed. The Gantt Progress Chart enables the manager to keep before him all the promises he has made, to concentrate his attention on overcoming obstacles and avoiding delays, and, when it is impossible to live up to a promise, it enables him to give the customer advance notice of the fact.

Drawing the Progress Chart

Angles opening to the right and to the left indicate respectively when the work is to be begun and completed. The amount of work scheduled is shown by a figure at the left of the space and the amount to be done to date by a figure at the right of the space; light lines represent work done during any period of time and heavy lines the amount done to date, as explained in Figures 1, 2, and 3 in Chapter I.

If work is done in a period of time for which no work was scheduled, it is shown by a figure in the middle of the space, for instance:

When the amount of work done is more than that scheduled, the light line is drawn across the space more than once, thus:

These lines are built up from the bottom to emphasize the fact that they belong to the heavy line below them. If no work is done in a period for which some was scheduled a **Z** (for zero) is placed in the middle of the space; thus:

| z |

A chart will look crowded if more than three light lines are drawn, so when the number of lines exceeds three, the figure is shown thus:

This indicates that the work done was seven times as great as the amount scheduled.

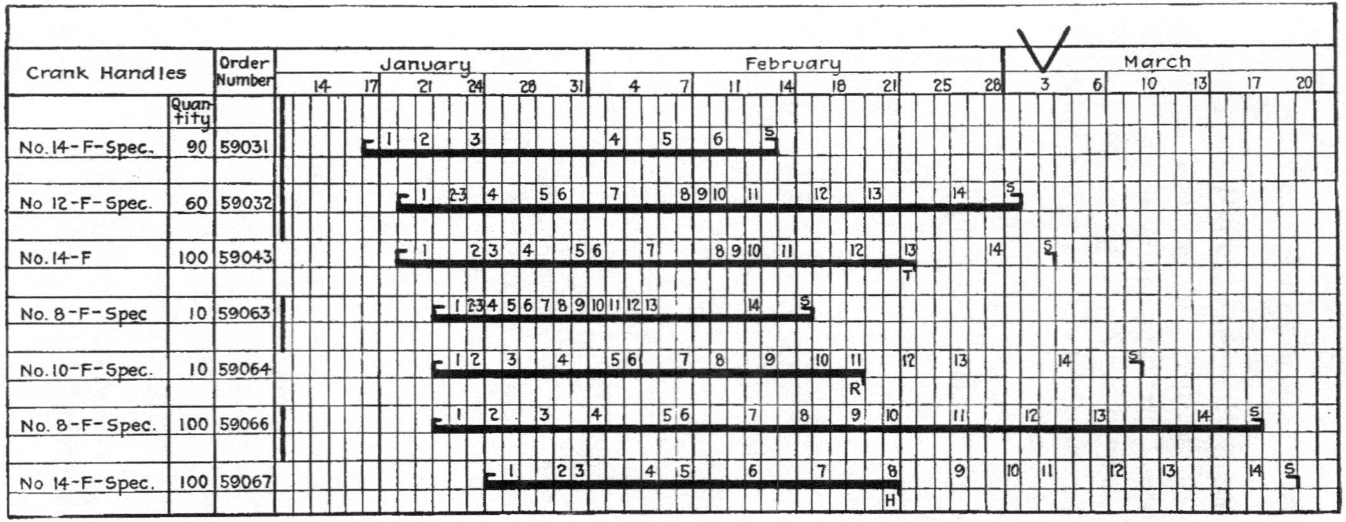

FIGURE 24. A GANTT PROGRESS CHART USED IN A PLANT WHICH MANUFACTURES ON ORDER

In this chart the angle opening to the right indicates the date on which the material was to be issued from stores; the figures indicate the operations to be done on the order and are placed under the dates on which they were to be begun; the angle opening to the left indicates the date on which the parts were to be shipped. The heavy lines show what operations have been done; and the letters under the lines indicate the reasons for delay. The *V* indicates that this chart was reproduced on March 3.

86

The heavy cumulative lines are drawn on the scale of the space through which they pass. Therefore, if the scale of the spaces or periods of time varies, the sum of the light lines may not equal the length of the cumulative line, as is the case in Man and Machine Record Charts.

Broken lines represent work which has been done previous to the date when the chart is drawn. If, for instance, a chart is to show quantities of parts manufactured, a heavy broken line would indicate the quantity in stock when the chart was begun.

Manufacturing on Order

In a plant which manufactures only on orders from its customers or its own sales organization, a promise of delivery is usually made on each order and each must be watched to see that the promise is kept. The Progress Chart of Crank Handles (Figure 24) was drawn in a plant where all orders were charted. The angle which opens to the right indicates the date on which the material was to be issued from stores; the figures indicate the dates on which the various operations are to be begun, that is, on the first line of the chart, 1 indicates that the first operation was to be begun on January 19, operation No. 2 on the 21st, etc.; the angle which opens to the left indicates the date on which the parts were to be shipped, the heavy line shows what operations have been done, and the letters under the lines indicate the reasons for delay.

The V indicates that this chart was reproduced on March 3. If the work had proceeded exactly according to schedule, the heavy lines would all end under that

Links Manufactured on Schedule

PART NO.	1921 June	July	Aug.	Sept.	Oct.	Nov.	Dec.	1922 Jan.	Feb.	Mar.	Apr.	May
467–BT												
Normal Usage	10M	20M	30M	40M	50M	60M	70M	80M	90M	100M	110M	120M
Actual Sales												
Received in Stock												
Manufacturing Orders Placed												
Forgings Received												
1297–BP												
Normal Usage	4M	8M	12M	16M	20M	24M	28M	32M	36M	40M	44M	48M
Actual Sales												
Received in Stock												
Manufacturing Orders Placed												
Forgings Received												
1463–BR												
Normal Usage	1200	2400	3600	4800	6000	7200	8400	9600	10800	12M	13200	14400
Actual Sales												
Received in Stock												
Manufacturing Orders Placed												
Forgings Received												

To Oct. 1922

88

FIGURE 25. A GANTT PROGRESS CHART USED IN A PLANT WHERE MANUFACTURE IS CONTINUOUS

LEGEND

|10M | Figure at left of monthly space is amount scheduled for each month.

|30M| Figure at right is amount to be done to date.

——— Work done that month.

Z Zero production, i.e., no work done that month.

▪▪▪▪ Work done before June 1, when chart was drawn up.

▬▬▬ Work done when chart was copied, August 31.

This chart was drawn in a plant where parts were manufactured continuously. On the third part, No. 1463-BR, an investigation of the sales for previous years led them to believe that their usage for the following year would amount to 1,200 per month. The actual sales, however, fell below the estimate and during the first 3 months they amounted to less than 2 months' normal usage. The amount in stock when the chart was drawn was 960, as shown by the broken line. During June 1,050 had been received, in July 720, and in August 1,440, making the total received equal to 3½

months' normal usage, as shown by the heavy line. Part of this amount had been sold, but the amount actually in stock was the difference between the cumulative lines for sales and receipts in stock, which was about 1¾ months' usage.

On the next line, i.e., "manufacturing orders placed," the broken line indicates that on June 1, there were orders in the shop calling for 3½ months' supply. The light line Z shows that no orders were placed in June. The light lines in July and August, indicating the orders placed, carried the cumulative line 2½ months beyond the amount received in stock.

The number of forgings on hand June 1, covered the manufacturing orders placed, and during July an additional order was entered for 3½ months' supply.

All of these lines moved forward month by month and the difference in the lengths of the cumulative lines always showed the parts in stock, the parts on order, and the forgings on hand.

date except for those orders which were due to be completed before that date. However, the work had not made the expected progress; the third order on the sheet was a week behind schedule, the fifth about 2 weeks behind, the sixth 2 weeks ahead, and the seventh 10 days behind time.

From this chart the manager could see at a glance which orders were behind schedule. On the fifth order on the sheet, for instance, he could see that the eleventh operation had been begun but not finished, and the *R* showed that the delay was caused by repairs. Reference to the shop order told the manager what that operation was and the department in which it was being done. Over the telephone he found out in detail from the foreman the repairs needed and the probable date when that operation would be finished. The chart showed how much more time would be needed for the remaining operations, so that the manager could take whatever action he deemed wise to rush the work and he could advise his customers as to the probable date of delivery.

Continuous Manufacture

In a plant where articles are manufactured continuously, the Progress Chart is, of course, somewhat different from that used in a plant which manufactures on order. The chart of Links Manufactured on Schedule (Figure 25) illustrates this.

On the first type of link, No. 467-BT, it was found that the normal usage based on sales for the last two years with more weight given to recent months was 10,000 per month. The broken lines were the first ones entered on the chart; it was found that about 16,000 finished links were in stock, and accordingly a broken line was drawn through the first month and 60 per cent of the second month. It was also found that manufacturing orders were in the shop for 10,000 additional links, so a broken line was drawn through an amount of space representing 2.6 months, that is, 1.6 months for the links in stock, which, of course, had been covered by past orders, and 1 month for the uncompleted orders. An inventory showed that there were in the storeroom 30,000 forgings besides the 26,000 links in process or in finished stock. Accordingly, a line was drawn through 5.6 months to represent 56,000 forgings and links.

During the month of June, 7,000 links were sold and a light line was, therefore, drawn through 70 per cent of the space, with a cumulative line of the same length. Also 12,000 links were received in stock, so a light line was drawn through 120 per cent of the June space and a heavy line of equal length was added to the broken line. During the same month orders were placed for 27,500 links because the management had decided to build up a 4 months' stock and after that to manufacture each month an amount equal to the sales of the previous month. No forgings were received that month, so a Z was entered in the space.

During July and August, sales fell below the normal usage with the result that at the end of August, when the chart was reproduced, the difference between the cumulative line representing sales and the line representing receipts into stock showed the amount of links in stock, namely about 3½ months' supply. During August manufacturing orders had been entered

Brake   Week Ending Jan.25

Sheet No.1

| | MONDAY 20 | TUESDAY 21 | WEDNESDAY 22 | THURSDAY 23 | FRIDAY 24 | SATURDAY 25 |

Sheet No.1	OP. NO.
Laying Out	1
Rough Plane	2
Rough Plane	2A
Mill Accurate	3
Plane	4
Rough Plane	4A
Finish Plane	5
Rough Plane	6
Finish Plane	6A
Drill	7
Drill	8
Rough Ream	9
Rough Ream	10
Rough Plane	11
Rough Plane	12
Rough Plane	13
Rough Turn	14
Finish Mill	15
Mill	16
Mill	17
Finish Plane	18
Finish Plane	18A
Finish Mill	19
Finish Mill	20

No. Fixture – Combined with Oper. 6A

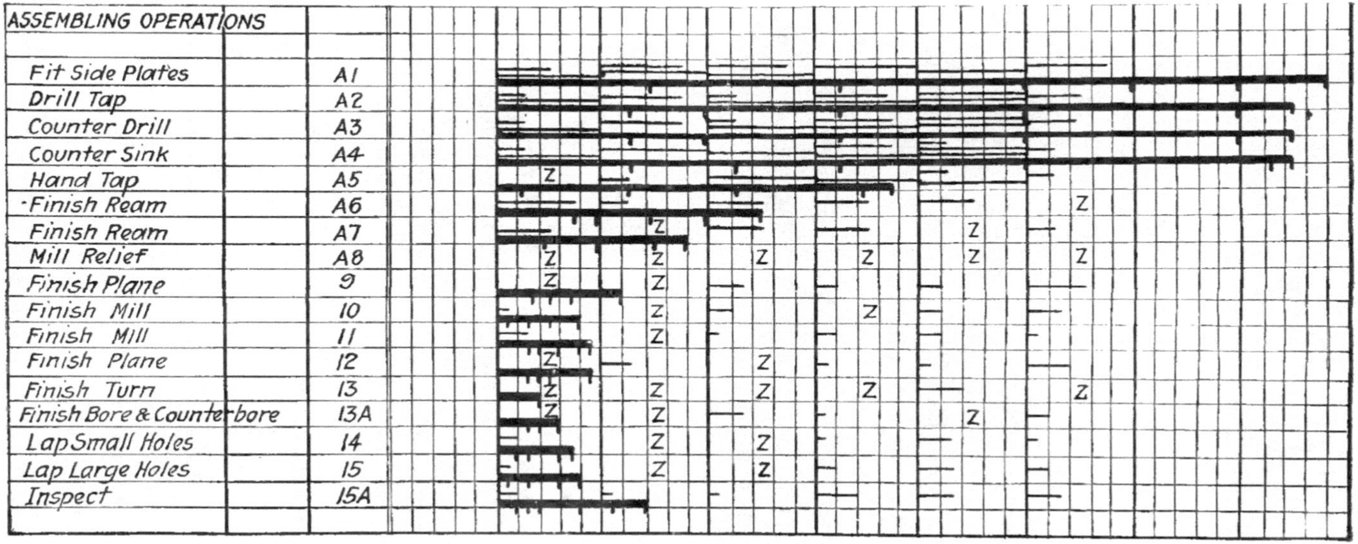

FIGURE 26. PROGRESS OF WORK THROUGH VARIOUS OPERATIONS

On this chart is shown a week's work on the various operations done on a brake. In order to get out the required production it was necessary to build 4 brakes per day on each operation and the necessary machine tools had been provided with this end in view. The lines show that on some operations more than a week's work had been done, while on others very little had been accomplished. The short lines indicated which operations were causing the most trouble and directed the attention of the management to the necessity for overcoming those difficulties. The tapping and reaming, operations A5, 6, and 7, were causing serious delay.

which would bring into finished stock during September another month's supply. It was evident, therefore, that there would be a 4 months' supply on hand sometime in September, and accordingly no further manufacturing orders were placed. It was also evident that there were sufficient forgings on hand so that no further purchase orders were necessary.

On the next type of link, No. 1297-BP, the normal usage was 4,000 per month. When the chart was made up June 1, 5 months' supply was already in stock with manufacturing orders placed for 15,000 more and forgings on hand sufficient to last up to October of the following year. The chart made it clear that it was unnecessary to place additional orders for the manufacture of links or for forgings.

Comparing Operations

At times a series of delays occur which interfere seriously with production, but it is difficult to get a comprehensive understanding of the situation from a table of figures and still more difficult to explain it to someone who is not familiar with the details.

During the latter part of the Great War, the Director of Arsenals considered the recuperators, or recoil mechanisms, for the 75mm. field guns the most important work in American arsenals. There had been a number of delays on this work with various explanations given and finally the director asked to have the progress shown on a Gantt chart. Figure 26 shows the progress made during a certain week on the framework of the recuperator, usually called the "brake," and compares that progress with the schedules.

A large machine shop had been erected and machine tools installed to manufacture these recuperators at the rate of 4 per day. The chart shows that on the first operation 5 were done on Monday and Tuesday, 4 on Wednesday, and none the remainder of the week. The production for the week was, therefore, 2½ out of 6 days. Going through the various operations it was evident at a glance that the principal delays were occurring on operations 4A and 5, planing, and on A6 and A7, reaming, and that on the remaining operations little or nothing was being done. This chart focused the attention of the management on those operations and made apparent to everyone concerned the relative importance of this delay.

Office Work

The work of an office is usually more difficult to measure than that of a shop, but it can be done in nearly all cases. Office departments usually have a few things around which their other work revolves; in an advertising department, for instance, they have several individuals whose duty it is to get out circular letters. It is easy to decide on a daily task of a certain number of letters. Another group in this same department may be answering inquiries, and since no one knows in advance how many inquiries will be received each day, no one can say how many should be answered. However, it is most important to have those inquiries handled promptly, so the real task of this group of people is to answer each day all the inquiries received. Their daily task is then expressed in numbers of inquiries received.

	MON.	TUES.	WED.	THURS.	FRI.	SAT.	MON.
ORDER DEPT.							
ORDERS FOR "A"	420	260	320	410	380	220	
" " "B"	80	46	60	70	65	55	
" " "C"	152	94	126	104	210	142	
SHIPMENTS CHECKD	504	620	652	534	422	268	
TRAFFIC DEPT.							
SHIPMENTS ROUTED	462	416	358	390	424	306	
FRT BILLS CHECKED.	246	275	309	213	280	204	
BILLING DEPT.							
SHIPMENTS BILLED.	632	580	608	539	470	349	
PURCHASING DEPT.							
ORDERS PLACED	46	72	64	30	56	20	
" FILLED	84	78	106	92	68	54	

FIGURE 27. PROGRESS CHART OF OFFICE WORK

It is the aim of an office manager to get work done, and in order to accomplish this he wants to know at frequent intervals, usually daily, what progress is being made. Accordingly, he gets reports from each of his department heads showing the amount of work they receive each day, the amount done, and the amount left over at the end of the day. He has one of his assistants enter this information on a chart and by 10 o'clock each morning show him a complete record of the previous day's performance.

In this particular office each day's job consisted of the work received up to 3 o'clock that day. The figures at the left of each space represent the number of orders, etc., received day by day. The lines represent the amount of work done, the light ones showing daily production and the heavy ones the amounts done since the beginning of the week.

Taking, for instance, the orders for "A" on Monday, 420 orders were received; 252 were passed through to the shop; 252 is 60 per cent of 420, so a light line is drawn through 60 per cent of the space for Monday. A heavy line is drawn below the light line to indicate the cumulative work done.

This chart is so simple that anyone in the office can understand it; it emphasizes above everything else the time when the work should be finished; and shows at a glance what work is up to date and what work is behind.

The daily task in most office departments can be expressed in one of these two ways, i.e., by a definite quantity per day or by the amount of work received each day. Of course, it is impossible to get out at closing time, say, 5 o'clock, work which is not received until 10 minutes before 5, but the day for receiving work may be regarded as ending at 3 o'clock or possibly at noon, while the day for finishing work may not end until 5 o'clock.

In a purchasing department, for instance, the task may be to send out requests for quotations or purchase orders by 5 o'clock, covering all requisitions received up to 3 o'clock. The task of a stenographic department would be to transcribe before closing time all letters dictated before 4 o'clock. The filing department's task would be to get into their proper places in the files all papers secured from the various office departments at 9 o'clock that morning.

In order to get things done on time in an office, a department head or office manager must be kept advised continually and promptly as to whether or not those under his control are doing their work on time. It is also his duty to maintain a definite standard of quality in the work turned out, but that is not quite so difficult as to keep the work up to date. A Progress Chart such as is illustrated in Figure 27 keeps an office manager accurately and promptly advised as to the status of the work under his charge and enables him to give whatever assistance may be necessary to those behind schedule.

Sales Quotas

During the last decade sales quotas have come into such general use that it is no longer necessary to point

out the advantages of giving a salesman a definite task.
In most well-managed sales companies today the
managers and salesmen sit down together and agree
upon what will be a fair quota for each territory or individual. However, a satisfactory method of showing a
comparison between actual sales and quotas is not so
generally understood and unless this comparison is constantly brought to the attention of those responsible for
sales, much of the value of the quota plan is lost.

The Progress Chart of Sales Quotas (Figure 28)
shows how the sales of one company in the various
districts of the United States compared with the quotas.
It is evident from the chart that the sales from the
southern and southwestern states had fallen very far
below what was expected and the attention of the
management was turned toward an investigation of the
reasons for the poor business in those states.

Storeskeeping

In keeping materials or finished goods in stores,
time is the most important feature to be taken into consideration, and any analysis of conditions in a storeroom must be expressed in terms of days, months, or
years as well as in quantities. Information that there
are 1,000 pieces on hand is not of nearly so much value
as that there are enough pieces on hand to last a year at
the normal rate of usage.

The chart illustrated in Figure 29 compares the
stock on hand at the first of the year with the average
sales of the 5 previous years. It is possible to see at a
glance that they were out of stock of one item, that on
two others they had less than a week's supply; and that

SALES – ARTICLE "A" – Cartons

	JAN.	FEB.	MAR.	APR.	MAY	JUNE	JULY	AUG.	SEPT.	OCT.	NOV.	DEC.
	840	1400 1200	2100 800	3600 500	4600 400	4550 900	5400 540	6600 1260	7200 240	7400 270	7500 570	8000
UNITED STATES TOTAL												
New England	109	154 254	546 148	718 112	800 52	912 178	1090 106	1196 240	1436 34	1472 109	1572 20	1592
North Atlantic	119	126 274	552 126	591 116	659 82	936 190	1116 14	1240 248	1448 40	1528 104	1632 32	1664
Eastern	78	54 118	254 80	334 60	354 56	410 82	502 40	510 110	590 18	678 48	724 10	734
Southern	128	90 186	410 126	226 82	608 50	616 132	736 76	814 178	1048 30	1078 72	1150 14	1164
Central	72	52 104	292 74	306 42	354 34	388 22	454 48	510 102	612 16	620 42	670 10	680
Southwestern	130	84 182	380 122	342 76	590 56	642 126	772 78	848 170	1016 30	1048 70	1116 14	1132
Northwestern	56	42	98 84	176 68	244 40	254 21	312	314 38	412 82	494 14	508 34	542 6	548
Western	52	36	90 60	170 52	222	260 24	260 50	336 34	370 74	444 16	450 32	492 4	496

FIGURE 28.   PROGRESS CHART FOR SALES QUOTAS

The sales quotas for article *A* were subject to seasonal variation, which differed in each section of the United States. These quotas were worked out from records of past sales and a forecast of business conditions during the year. The quotas for individual territories were summed up into quotas for sections, such as New England, North Atlantic, etc., and the monthly amounts entered at the left of the space for that month. The light lines compare the monthly sales with the quotas.

The heavy lines indicate the progress made toward meeting the quotas up to the end of July. It will be seen at a glance that the southern and southwestern territories had fallen far behind their quotas and had wiped out the substantial gains made in four of the other territories.

The heavy line at the top of the sheet shows that the sales in the United States as a whole were about 200 cartons behind the quota.

This chart gives the executive a clear and comprehensive picture of the progress made in the work for which he is responsible. Where sales have been particularly poor, as indicated by short lines, he consults additional charts, showing territories divided into smaller units.

Stock on Hand, January 1st, 1921; Compared with One Year's Sales (An Average of Five Previous Years)

Part Number	Condition	Total on Hand	1st Quarter	(date)
705 A	Unfinished	1102	252	MAR 1925
	Semi-Fin.	1276	1655	
	Finished	1060	990	
5	Unfinished	100	140	
	Semi-Fin.	150	1075	
	Finished	150	210	MAY 1929
707	Unfinished	2849	338	
	Semi-Fin.	3611	2742	AUG 1925
	Finished	3250	780	
721	Unfinished	425	800	
	Semi-Fin.	5696	4000	
	Finished	6056	4800	
21-6	Unfinished	6	840	
	Semi-Fin.	125	780	
	Finished	3	340	JULY 1927
32	Unfinished	1710	260	
	Semi-Fin	5369	4400	
	Finished	2800	3600	SEPT 1973
33	Unfinished	5564	2100	
	Semi-Fin.	13083	8000	
	Finished	5780	7200	
33 C	Unfinished	76	200	
	Semi-Fin	6930	4800	MAR 1928
	Finished	2871	3600	
732	Unfinished	409	50	
	Semi-Fin	342	410	
	Finished	532	780	
735	Unfinished	336	540	
	Semi-Fin.	1223	7000	MAY 1929
	Finished	1410	8000	
33-24	Unfinished	100	30	
	Semi-Fin	0	140	SEPT 2004
	Finished	100	240	FEB 1928
135	Unfinished	807	70	DEC 1924
	Semi-Fin	2851	400	
	Unfinished	3200	800	

FIGURE 29. PROGRESS CHART SHOWING UNBALANCED CONDITIONS OF STORES

This chart was used in analyzing the stock on hand in a manufacturing plant. At the left of the sheet the part numbers were listed. Each was kept in stock and sold in three kinds of finish. In the next column was entered the total number of parts on hand. The figures at the left of the space for 1921 indicated the normal yearly sale of these parts. For instance, on the first line we see that the yearly usage of part No. 705 A, unfinished, amounted to 252. The number on hand was 1,102, which at the rate of 252 per year, would last until March, 1925. A heavy line was, therefore, drawn through 3 years on the chart and a note was placed at the right to indicate how much longer these parts could be expected to last.

On the next line we see that in semifinished condition there was about 9 months' stock on hand.

Glancing down the chart, it will be noticed that the stock was in an unbalanced condition, some items being out of stock, while others were seriously overstocked, the extreme case being part No. 135, unfinished, which at the normal rate of usage, would last for a period of 80 years.

on 10 items they had more than enough to last for 3 years. In one extreme case, where the usage was small, they had enough to last for 80 years.

For the analysis of a situation of this kind no table of figures or form of chart can convey the information in so illuminating or compact a way as the Gantt Progress Chart.

Budgets and Expenses

The ability of an executive is judged to a considerable extent by the cost of doing the work assigned to him. The best way to control expenditures is to keep continually before those who authorize them a comparison between what they are spending and what they should spend. The Gantt chart presents such records more clearly and concisely than can be done on any other type of chart or by any table of figures. A comparison of actual expenses with predetermined expense in a foundry is shown in Figure 30. The first line indicates that in January the total expenses of the foundry amounted to about 90 per cent normal, and in February 60 per cent. The succeeding lines show which departments have been within the budget and which have exceeded it.

A Public Service Plant

The amount of coal loaded into ships by a large coal pier belonging to an eastern railway was not considered satisfactory. This was one of the finest coal piers on the Atlantic coast and it appeared to be in good repair. The pier was known to be capable of dumping more than 40,000 tons per day, so that figure was taken as the capacity of the pier and official reports for 2 weeks were charted (Figure 31). The "amount actually dumped" into vessels was first charted; on the first day, the 20th, 12,000 tons were dumped, which was 30 per cent of the pier's capacity. The chart made it clear that in 2 weeks an amount of coal was dumped into vessels which could have been dumped in 3 days, if the capacity of the pier had been used.

It was natural to expect that as soon as this fact was presented the excuse would be advanced that larger quantities of coal had not been dumped either because there had been no more coal in the yards or because there had been no more vessels in the harbor ready to be loaded. Therefore information was taken from official reports and entries were made on the chart to show how much coal was in the yards which served the pier and the tonnage (the coal-carrying capacity) of the vessels available at the end of the day.

It was apparent from this chart that the amount of coal dumped into vessels had not been limited at any time by a shortage of coal in the yards or of vessels to receive it, and that the responsibility for the failure of this pier even to approach its capacity was due to the management of the pier itself.

Charts for Executives

Modern business is so complicated that unless an executive takes effective steps to prevent it, he will be so overwhelmed by detail that he will not be able to discharge the real duties of his office. Gantt charts intelligently handled will go far toward clearing his desk for action. They will greatly reduce the writing

		JAN.	FEB.	MAR.	APR.	MAY	JUNE	JULY	AUG.	SEPT.	OCT.	NOV.	DEC.
TOTAL FOUNDRY	F	$53,910	69M	102M	95M	112M	203M	237M	271M	303M	333M	373M	407M
TOTAL BUILDING EXPENSE	C	5380	1M	1M	2M	27M	25M	39M	4.1M	49M	5M	53M	6M
Depreciation	C D	850	4.1M	1.9M	3.2M	3.1M	3.2M	4.3M	5M	5.6M	6.2M	68M	7.4M
Supervision	C E	2.60	1M	61M	12M	10M	12M	14M	16M	19M	21M	23M	25M
Maintenance	C M	850	2.5M	3.1M	49M	62M	7.4M	8.6M	9.4M	11M	12M	14M	15M
Insurance	C N	700	810		9M	8.4M	1.7M	1.4M	1.3M	1.4M	1.4M	1.8M	1.9M
Repairs	C R	2M	6.5M	5.5M	1M	45M	1.8M	1.9M	2.1M	2.4M	2.5M	3M	3.2M
Taxes	C T	4000	2M	3M	4.1M	5.1M	6.1M	7.1M	8.2M	9.2M	10M	11M	12M
TOTAL DIRECT DEPTS	D	42,200	5.1M	138M	105M	151M	151M	183M	210M	236M	262M	288M	314M
Pattern House	D-51	850	2M	3.1M	4.3M	6.3M	6.3M	7.3M	8.4M	9.5M	11M	12M	13M
Large Cores	D-52	3100	6.6M	9.2M	3M	3M	10M	23M	26M	30M	33M	36M	40M
Small Cores	D-53	2.50	4.3M	6.5M	8.4M	11M	13M	15M	17M	19M	22M	24M	26M
Crane Floor	D-54	2100	5.1M	8M	11M	14M	17M	20M	20M	25M	28M	31M	34M
Side Floor	D-55	2.5M	4.9M	20M	9M	12M	14M	17M	20M	22M	25M	27M	29M
Bench Floor	D-56	2.9M	4.1M	6.1M	9M	11M	14M	16M	18M	20M	23M	25M	27M
Steel Floor	D-57	2.00	42M	28M	10M	13M	16M	18M	21M	23M	26M	25M	31M
Brass Floor	D-58	590	1M	14M	2M	2M	3M	35M	4M	45M	5M	53M	6M
Brass Melting	D-58-3	8M	2.4M	3.3M	2M	51M	64M	74M	8.3M	5.2M	11M	12M	13M
Brass Cleaning	D-58-3	570	1.7M	2.4M	5.3M	24M	3.1M	3.6M	4.2M	47M	5.2M	57M	6.2M
Steel Melting	D-59	190	2.4M	1.4M	53M	13M	87M	10M	12M	13M	15M	16M	17M
Iron Melting	D-60	1140	3.7M	5.1M	7M	92M	11M	13M	15M	17M	18M	20M	22M
Iron Cleaning	D-61A	2.9M	6.4M	8.1M	11M	14M	17M	20M	23M	25M	28M	31M	34M
Steel Cleaning	D-61C	1.40	2.1M	43M	5.6M	7M	8.4M	9.2M	11M	13M	14M	15M	17M
Indirect Dept's	D I	2.240	52M	7M	7M	12M	14M	16M	19M	2M	21M	24M	29M

to 2-16 '23

FIGURE 30. PROGRESS CHART USED TO DETERMINE SHOP COSTS

This chart was used in a foundry where costs were applied to work done by means of floor rates, that is, a certain amount per hour for each molding floor. These rates were based on predetermined costs, i.e., past records of expenses were studied and estimates made as to what expenses would be in the future. These costs were, of course, estimated, and it was important to compare the actual money spent with these estimates, so the estimates were used as the schedule and the figures written on the chart. The lines represent the actual money spent.

The cost of insurance was much higher than had been expected, but the expenses chargeable to the core rooms and molding floors had been kept well below the estimates. Most of the items of actual expense varied considerably from the estimates and the chart showed that the estimates themselves were high, for in 7 months the amount spent was only slightly in excess of the predetermined costs for 4 months. When such a chart is put into the hands of the men who authorize expenditures, the usual result is a wiser and more careful handling of expenses.

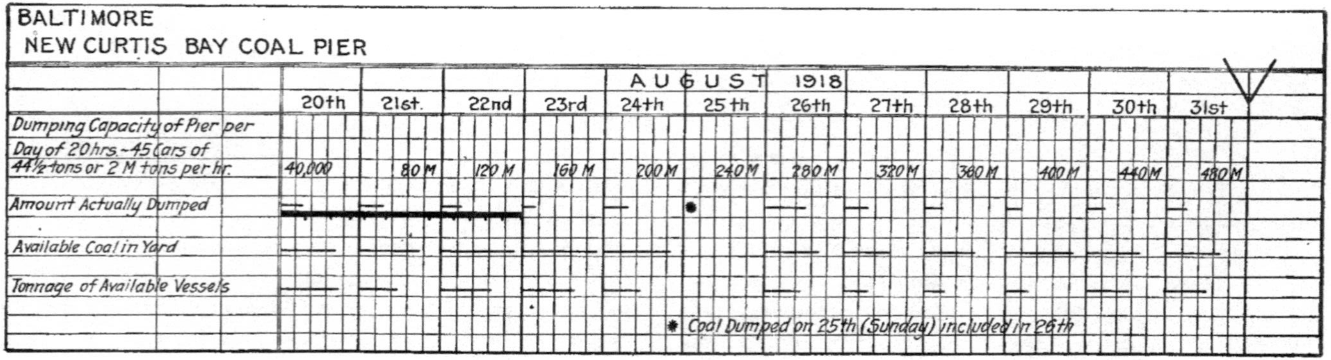

FIGURE 31. A PUBLIC SERVICE PLANT

This is a chart showing the operation of a coal pier. Records had made it clear that the dumping capacity of this pier was in excess of 40,000 tons per day. Reports of amounts actually dumped each day showed that they averaged about 25 per cent of the capacity. The heavy cumulative line made it clear that in 2 weeks the amount dumped equaled the capacity for 3 days.

One of the things most likely to limit the dumping of coal was the amount of available coal in the yard. This was, therefore, charted on the second line.

The next thing likely to limit the capacity was the tonnage of the vessels ready to receive the coal. This was accordingly charted on the third line. It was clear that in every case there was an abundance of coal in the yards and on only one day, the 27th, the dumping was limited by the capacity of available vessels.

of letters and wordy reports; they will make it easy to discover inaccuracies in reports; they will make clear what is to be done and what has been done.

Since the task of an executive is to get work done and the Gantt Progress Chart compares the work done with what was planned, it is evident that this chart provides a method of measuring the service rendered by an executive. It is no longer necessary to depend upon general impressions in judging the ability of an executive, since by the use of the Gantt chart executive ability is capable of being fairly accurately measured.

CHAPTER IX

CHARTING THE AMERICAN MERCHANT MARINE

The Shipping Problem During the War

During the war years of 1917 and 1918 Gantt charts were of great value in getting things done in the Ordnance Department, the Navy, the Emergency Fleet, the Shipping Board, and other government departments. The following account of how the Gantt chart was applied to the handling of ships will show how it simplifies problems of the greatest magnitude and complexity.

Even before the entrance of the United States into the war, shipping had undergone great changes; the number of ships at sea had been greatly decreased by losses due to submarines and raiders and by the internment of German vessels; the production of foodstuffs in allied countries had suddenly decreased, causing a greater demand for the transportation of food from overseas; the increased production of war materials in Europe created a greater demand for raw materials and consequently more ships to carry them; the menace of the submarine made it necessary to convoy all vessels approaching or leaving Europe, causing untold delay; the submarine also drove all sailing vessels and all slow steamers from the North Atlantic. The concentration of millions of men on a narrow front in France focused the shipping of the world on that point and overtaxed existing docking facilities. All these circumstances combined to cause a shortage of shipping at a most critical time.

As soon as the United States entered the war, steps were taken to build more ships. The Shipping Board was created and it formed a subsidiary organization called the "Emergency Fleet Corporation" to build ships, but the board itself operated them. The period of time which necessarily had to elapse before new ships could be built made the use of the existing ships even more important, if that were possible, than the building of new ones. The ships already at sea were, of course, going to whatever ports and carrying whatever cargoes the ship-owners found most profitable. Consequently, it became necessary for the Shipping Board to commandeer all vessels owned or leased by Americans and to charter as many additional vessels as possible from foreign nations.

First Methods of Keeping Ship Records

The handling of this large and ever-growing fleet was a stupendous task—probably the most difficult problem which had ever arisen in the shipping world.

It was found impossible at first even to keep track of the movements of vessels in general, to say nothing of determining whether they were on the right jobs and doing their work efficiently. For a time there was little progress. The old plan of tracing ships by sticking pins and flags on large maps was tried, but it was soon discovered that this system with its thousands of pins and flags was so cumbersome that it was impossible to follow the movements of even coastwise vessels. The most serious limitation of this system was that it did not take any account of time—a flag bearing the name of a steamer and stuck in a port gave no information as to how long the steamer had been there or where it had been before that.

Card records were next tried, but there was such a mass of information and it was so difficult to secure any comprehensive idea of its tendencies or to visualize what was happening that the information remained buried in the files.

At this point Mr. Gantt was called in. He first worked out a simple method of visualizing what the ships were doing day by day by means of ship movement charts of which some typical specimens are described below.

Ship Movement Charts

A right angle opening to the right indicated that the "Vesta" arrived in Baltimore on the 27th, coming from Port Arthur, Texas, loaded with oil (Figure 32). She left Baltimore on the 28th and reached Nor-

FIGURE 32. MOVEMENTS OF TANKER "VESTA"

folk on the 2nd, sailing from there on the 3rd in ballast. After 6 days at sea, she arrived at Port Arthur and sailed from there on the 12th with oil for Norfolk.

The "Kronstad," a Norwegian vessel chartered by

the United States government, sailed from New York
with a general cargo and on the 14th arrived at Car-
denas, on the north coast of Cuba, dropping anchor in
the roadstead because she drew too much water to enter
the harbor or tie up to the wharf (Figure 33). By the

12		16		19		23	26		30		3			7
NEW YORK GEN'L	CAR- DENAS	CAI- BARIEN	SUGAR			N.Y.		BOSTON			NEW YORK			

10		14	17		21	24		28	31		4
NORFOLK	COAL		MATANZAS	SUGAR		NEW YORK			BOSTON		CUBA BAL.

FIGURE 33.   MOVEMENTS OF SS. "KRONSTAD"

next day she had loaded all the sugar in the warehouses,
but her hold was not yet filled, so she weighed anchor
and steamed to Caibarien and took on enough to make
a full cargo.

On the 18th, the "Kronstad" sailed for New York,
which she reached on the 24th. After discharging part
of her cargo at a refinery there, she steamed up through
the Sound to Boston, where she discharged the remainder of the sugar. She then came back to New
York for a general cargo, but not being able to pick
up enough to fill up her holds, she went down to Norfolk and took on coal.

On the 15th, the "Kronstad" steamed into the harbor of Matanzas where she lay at anchor 4 days while
bags of sugar were loaded from lighters. On the 24th,
she was back in New York, on the 30th at Boston, and
on the 2nd she sailed for Cuba in ballast.

8

Ship schedule chart — JANUARY / FEBRUARY

	FLAG	JAN 1	5	8	12	15	19	22	26	29	FEB 2	5	9	12	16	19	23	
Runa	Nor.				CHILE	NEW ORLEANS	NORFOLK								BALBOA	IQUIQUE		
Salonica	Nor.		CANAL	NEW YORK			NORFOLK			PERU-COAL	CANAL				MOLLENDO			
San Francisco	Am.	VALPARAISO		TALCA	CORRAL NITRATE	IQUIQUE					NITRATE	BALBOA COLON		NITRATE	PHILADELPHIA			
Santa Alicia	Am						MOLLENDO	ARICA-ORES			VALP.	COQUIMBO-ORES MEJ	ANTOF'- ORES & NITRATE	TALLARA				
Santa Barbara	Am.			SENILOKLETA			COLON BALBOA	SAVANNAH								GONE TO ARMY		
Santa Inez	Am.		ANTOFEUS					TALLARA	S.F. NITRATE & ORES				PERII SAN PEDRO	S.F. TACOMA - NITRATE			
Santa Rita	Am.			CALLAO					MOLLENDO	ARICA			TALLARA			
Sara	Dan.	NORFOLK						VALPARAISO	N.Y.							OFF NITRATE		
Seaborn	Am.																
Sherman	Am.			NORFOLK	BALTIMORE		NEW YORK - ERIE BASIN						TOCAPILLA	CANAL	65 N'L		
Sinaloa	Nor.	NORFOLK			ANTOFOGASTA		TOCOPILLA							NITRATE S.F.			
Stegelborg	Dan.					ANTOF COAL	ANTOFOGASTA COAL	COLON-BALBOA									
St Paul	Am.									MITRATE LIVERPOOL N.Y. 80 TONS						
Strinda	Nor.		CANAL		IQUIQUE	PHILADELPHIA		NEW YORK				NEW YORK				OFF NITRATE		
Terrier	Nor.			CANAL	CHILE	NEW ORLEANS		COLON-BALBOA	CHILE BALBOA			TALTAL					
Thorgerd	Nor.	12/2 NT. VALPARISO- GENERAL			NEW ORLEANS		ANTOFOGASTA BALBOA COLON					CHARLESTON	NEW YORK				
Thyra S.	Dan.						JUCARA	CUBA NEW YORK									
Ujina	Br.	NORFOLK					NEWPORT-NITRATE									GONE TO WEST INDIES		

114

FIGURE 34. SHIP MOVEMENT CHART

LEGEND

Arrival in port.

⌐ Departure from port.

[Time spent in port.

If either angle is omitted, information is lacking as to date of arrival or departure.
Name to left of arrival—port of origin.
Name to right of departure—port of destination.
To right of destination—cargo carried.

The purpose of these Ship Movement Charts was to keep all information in regard to the locations and movements of vessels in one place where they would be available to everyone entitled to the information. It was possible to learn from this record where a vessel was, what she had done in the past, and what she was expected to do in the future.

This chart had an advantage over other types of records because it visualized the passing of time, inaccurate reports showed up plainly since a vessel could not be in two places at the same time, and past records could be entered under their proper dates instead of at the end of a list of later movements, as on a card record.

The most noticeable fact brought out by this chart was the length of time the vessels spent in United States harbors frequently due to congestion of docks, but more often due to lack of instructions as to what they were to do next. These vessels also spent a great deal of time going from one Chilean port to another picking up part of a cargo in each port.

To summarize: In the 53 days from April 10 to June 2 the "Kronstad" spent 18 days at sea on two round trips to Cuba, 9 days in sugar ports, and 27 days in and around United States ports discharging and picking up cargoes, and this at a time when the American people were on rigorous sugar rations.

These Ship Movement Charts showed the facts clearly, with few words and in little space. The number of ships whose movements were recorded in this way (see Figure 34) was rapidly increased until the arrivals and departures of 12,000 vessels were kept on record.

Harbor Performance Charts

While the movements of vessels from port to port were being followed in New York and Baltimore, charts were being made of what the vesssels were doing in port day by day. Of these harbor performance charts the following are typical:

A certain British steamer with a general cargo from

	15	16	17	18	19	20	21	22	23	24	25	
General												General
Liverpool												Liverpool

FIGURE 35. CHART OF A BRITISH STEAMER IN HARBOR OF BALTIMORE

Liverpool entered the harbor of Baltimore on the 15th, as is indicated by the angle opening to the right (Figure 35). She went immediately to her berth and began discharging her cargo the same day. The light line shows that the unloading took a little over 3 days and was completed on the 18th. On the 19th she filled her bunkers with coal and began loading on the 20th, as is shown by the heavy line. On the 25th she sailed with a general cargo for Liverpool.

This was a good record, for she had been in the harbor only 9 full days and in that time she had discharged her cargo, bunkered, and loaded another cargo without a single idle day.

Contrast that record with this (Figure 36):

	18	19	20	21	22	23	24	25.	26	27	28	29	30	31
Manganese Rio Janeiro					Stream							Ⓥ		Ⓥ
	1	2	3	4	5	6	7	8	9	10	11	12	13	14
			ⒹⒹ	⑇Ⓓ			Ⓜ		Ⓟ	Ⓟ	Ⓟ	Ⓟ	Ⓟ	Ⓟ
	15	16	17											
	Ⓟ	Ⓟ	⌐ Coal Rio Janeiro											

FIGURE 36.   CHART OF A DANISH SAILING SHIP IN HARBOR OF
BALTIMORE

On the 18th a large full-rigged ship, a Danish vessel, entered Baltimore harbor. She dropped anchor in Canton Hollow and waited for permission to move to a dock to unload.

She dried her sails, the sailmaker mended a few that had been strained off Hatteras, new ropes were spliced, the painters were busy on her hull—all sorts of odd jobs were done while she waited. After 11 days of idleness orders were received and a tug came alongside and she moved slowly to her pier. She spent the rest of that day unloading ballast from one of her holds, as shown by the circles for idleness and the V for ballast. The next morning a big force of longshoremen began unloading her cargo of 3,000 tons of manganese, which she had taken on at Rio.

The following day she spent waiting for ballast to keep her on an even keel and then for 2 days double shifts of men unloaded the remainder of the manganese. On the 3d a tug towed her to a shipyard and 2 days were spent on a repair to her hull. Saturday afternoon, the 4th, she was towed out of the repair yard. Sunday and Monday were spent taking on a cargo of coal for Rio; Tuesday no labor could be secured; Wednesday she completed loading the coal. Then she anchored in the harbor again and waited for permission to sail. For 8 days she tugged at her anchor before her orders came, then she dropped down the stream and started on her long voyage back to Rio.

To summarize: She had been in port 30 days; only 3 days had been used in discharging her cargo, 2 in repairs, and 3 in loading an outward cargo; she had been idle 22 days.

Here is another actual case in New York Harbor (Figure 37):

		23	24	25	26	27	28	1	2	3	4	5	6	7	8
Brazil	•⌐				Stream							⌐▬▬▬		Ⓩ	Ⓩ
												'NO.18 BROOKLYN			
		9	10	11	12	13	14	15	16	17	18	19	20	21	22
		Ⓒ	Ⓒ	Ⓒ▬▬▬			▬Ⓩ	▬▬	Ⓩ	Ⓧ	▬▬		Stream		
				'NO.4 C.H.K.											
		23	24	25	26	27	28	29	30	31	1				
					Stream						⌐▬•	Petro and Naptha		
												Rosario		

FIGURE 37. CHART OF A STEAMER IN NEW YORK HARBOR

On the 23rd a large steamer passed Sandy Hook, coming in from Brazil, anchored off the Statue of

Liberty, and waited for a pier 9 days. She then went to a Brooklyn dock and for a day and a half loaded a cargo; for 2 days she was idle for some unknown reason; 2½ days were spent in idleness because there was no more cargo ready to load. She then moved to a pier at Constable Hook; for 3 days she loaded case oil; she was idle for half a day; then loaded for a day and a half; and was idle again for a day and a half (Saturday afternoon and Sunday). She loaded for another day and half and then moved away from her pier and anchored off Tompkinsville. There she stayed idle for 10 days, waiting for her sailing orders.

This steamer had been in port 5 weeks and only 8 days had been spent in loading her cargo.

The Task of the Shipping Board

While this information as to the movement of ships both at sea and in port was being collected, Mr. Gantt was helping to solve the bigger problem of what the ships ought to be doing. The three jobs to be done were, in the order of their importance:

1. To carry troops, munitions, and supplies to France and food to the Allies in Europe.
2. To import into this country the necessary food and the raw materials needed for the manufacture of munitions.
3. To export to foreign countries the things they had to have in order to produce the raw materials needed by the United States.

The ships which carried troops, munitions, and supplies to France were operated by the army, but the ves-

sels under its control were inadequate. It was therefore important for the Shipping Board to bring in the
necessary imports with as few ships as possible and to
turn over all others to the army.

The export problem was also important; for instance, to get nitrate for munitions and agricultural
purposes from the mines of northern Chile, it was necessary to supply the coal and fuel oil needed to operate
the mines and the railroads which brought the nitrate
to the coast. Before manganese for armor-plate steel
could be brought from Brazil, coal had to be sent for
their railroads and coastwise shipping. If agricultural
machinery and coal were not shipped to the Argentine,
that country could not send wheat or meat to the Allies.
This problem was important, but it was not particularly
difficult, because export requirements were very much
smaller than import requirements and cargoes could be
carried out by vessels which were going after necessary
imports.

The Import Problem

The hardest task before the Shipping Board was this
import problem:

1. What had to be imported in order to manufacture munitions and to feed the people?
2. What raw materials produced in this country
   could be substituted for those which had heretofore been imported?
3. When would these things be needed by the various government departments, manufacturers,
   and consumers?

No one knew the answers to these questions and it seemed a superhuman task to secure such information. Nothing of the kind had ever been heard of in the shipping world, but nevertheless it was done. Experts were called together from universities, trade organizations, and government departments and they put into concrete form the task before the Shipping Board. About a hundred different commodities were found to be absolutely necessary and the amounts needed month by month were determined. The list was short but the quantities were staggering; 2,000,000 long tons of nitrate were required per year and between 3,000,000 and 4,000,000 tons of sugar. Moving such quantities in ships with average capacities of between 3,000 and 4,000 tons seemed impossible.

When the necessary commodities and the proper quantities had been determined, these requirements had to be translated into terms of individual ships and their cargoes:

1. What ships were available to bring in these imports?
2. What could they be expected to do per month or year?
3. What commodities could be secured from nearby countries which had heretofore been brought from ports several thousand miles away?

The lists of available ships were easily made up, but the answer to the second question was not so quickly arrived at. No two vessels seemed to do a job in the same way, so it was useless to estimate the time required

NITRATE IMPORTS 1918

SHEET NO.1	FLAG	NITRATE CAPACITY	JAN	FEB	MAR	APRIL	MAY	JUNE	JULY	AUG	SEPT	OCT	NOV	DEC
Requirements			178M	369M / 374M	466M / 515M	616M / 674M	650M / 824M	151M / 975M	135M / 1110M	116M / 1226M	137M / 1363M	149M / 1512M	144M / 1658M	1800M
Estimated Deliveries														
Actual Deliveries														
A.D. Bordes	Fr.	3383				3383								
Admiral Goodrich	Am.	1800												
Aitoku Maru	Jap.	3746												
Alice A Leigh	Br.	4788												
Almendral	Fr.	3200			363									
Alvarado	Am.	2300						2307						
Amsteldijk	Du.	8152						8152						
Ancom	Am.	10400												
Annam	Du.	9531												
Antoinette	Fr.	4000				3531								
Artemis	Nor.	9200						9200						
Asie	Fr.	4000				3530								
Astri	Nor.	3663												
Ataka Maru	Jap.	4640												
Awa Maru	Jap.	6456												
Alloway	Am.	7520												
Arganna	Am.	7100												
Anacortes	Am.	6000	1900											
Baja California	Nor.	2500				833			2500					
Batjan	Du.	8330					8330							
Bayamo	Am.	4565					2565							
Beatrice	Am.	4552					4552							
Bessegen	Nor.	4680					4680							
Borneo	Du.	8700					8700							
Bratland	Nor.	3300						1130						
Brighton	Nor.	1330							1300					
Bylgyl	Am.	5000			1200									
Belfast	Am.	2985												
Brynhild	Don.	3200												

FIGURE 38. SHIP CHART OF COMMODITIES

1,178M ⎧ Figures to left of monthly space show import requirements.

, 347M⎫ Figures to right of monthly space show cumulative requirements.

Light lines indicate monthly deliveries. The ratio of the length of the line to the monthly space is the same as the ratio of the deliveries to the requirements.

Heavy lines indicate cumulative deliveries.

Arrival in port.

6583 Long tons of nitrate delivered.

The purpose of this chart was to show the progress made toward meeting the requirements of nitrate, the actual and expected arrivals of vessels with the amounts of cargo carried, and the effect of allocating vessels to this trade or of taking them away from it.

The first heavy line at the top of the sheet shows that at the end of July sufficient vessels had been assigned to this trade to meet the requirements to the middle of November, although the actual deliveries, as shown by the lower line, were at that time 2 months behind schedule.

The first vessel on the list, the "A. D. Bordes," had arrived the second week in April with 3,383 tons of nitrate, which was a full cargo. The "Baja California," further down on the sheet, with a capacity of 2,500 tons had brought in 1,900 tons in January, 833 in April (the remainder of her capacity was taken up with copper), a full cargo of 2,500 tons in July, and was due to arrive the second week in October with another cargo.

At times during 1918 there were about 90 steam and sailing vessels on this nitrate trade.

for a "turnaround," as a round trip is called in shipping circles, by figuring the distance, the speed, and the possible time of loading. The only information which was of any value was a record of what had actually been done in the past. Accordingly, charts were drawn showing turnarounds based on averages of all voyages for which accurate records were available and they provided a fairly dependable basis for forecasting the dates on which vessels could be expected to discharge their cargoes.

Ship Charts of Commodities

One of the most important commodities to be brought into the country was nitrate, for it was used in the manufacture of nearly all explosives as well as for agricultural purposes, and neither the munitions nor the food programs could proceed without it. The large deposits in the northern part of Chile were the only source of supply and the nitrate was needed in the central and eastern states, so vessels had to come up the west coast of South America through the Panama Canal to Atlantic ports from Norfolk to Boston.

The quantities required varied from 178,000 long tons in January to 116,000 in August. These requirements were entered at the top of a chart (see Figure 38) and immediately below them were shown the estimated deliveries, i.e., the tons of nitrate which could be delivered by the vessels chartered for that purpose. The first charts for nitrate were made up in February, 1918, and they made it clear that the vessels then on the nitrate trade could not bring in more than half of the requirements. The charts caused the assignment of additional vessels to the trade, but the average turn-around to North Atlantic ports was 66 days. Consequently it was not until May that the arriving vessels unloaded anywhere near a month's supply. At the end of July sufficient vessels had been chartered to meet our requirements up to the middle of November and there was ample time to assign additional vessels to bring in the total yearly requirements.

The next line showed actual deliveries, which were, at the end of July, 2 months behind schedule.

Below these lines showing deliveries there was a list of steamers and sailing vessels on the nitrate trade. During a good part of the year over ninety vessels were engaged in this trade. The amount of nitrate which each ship could carry was shown alongside the name, and under the proper week and month an angle indicated the date of arrival and figures showed the tons of nitrate actually delivered. Angles without figures indicated expected arrivals.

Charts of this kind were made up for all of the commodities which were imported in large quantities. They showed the progress made toward meeting the requirements; they emphasized the necessity of allocating vessels to bring in specific commodities; and, when vessels were allocated, they showed what effect that action would have on meeting requirements.

Individual Commodity Charts

Many of the one hundred necessary commodities were brought in in part cargoes and from various parts of the world. In order to emphasize the savings in ships' time by importing from nearby countries, each

BEANS, CASTOR

IMPORTS IN LONG TONS 1918

	JAN.	FEB.	MAR.	APR.	MAY.	JUNE	JULY	AUG.	SEPT.	OCT.	NOV.	DEC.
TOTAL												
Requirements	8.5M	1.6M	2.5M	3.3M	4.1M	5M	5.8M	6.6M	7.5M	8.3M	9.1M	10M
Actual Deliveries										Surplus 10/10/19		
1 East Asian												
2 East Indian												
3 British Indian												
4 Australian												
5 Hawaiian												
6 Amazonian												
7 Central Brazilian												
8 La Plata												
9 Central Chilian												
10 North Chilian												
11 Peruvian												
12 Caribbean												
13 West Indies												
14 Mexican Gulf												
15 Pacific Mexico												
16 Arabian												
17 East African												
18 South African												
19 West African												
20 Mediterranean												
21 Levant												
22 Channel												
23 Scandinavian												
24 Arctic Russia												
25 Greenland												
26 Canadian Atlantic												
27 Canadian Pacific												

FIGURE 39. INDIVIDUAL COMMODITY CHART

|833 | Figures to left of monthly space show import requirements.

|OM| Figures to right of monthly space show cumulative requirements.

— | Light lines indicate monthly deliveries.

▬ | Heavy lines indicate cumulative deliveries.

Amounts received from the various trade regions are charted on the same scale as the total.

The purpose of this chart was to show the progress made toward meeting the requirements and what proportion of the total was received from each trade region. At the end of August enough castor beans had been received to meet the requirements up to October, 1919; in January, 8½ months' supply had been received; in February, 5½ months'; and in later months more moderate quantities. Most of the beans had been brought from across the Pacific and only small quantities from the Caribbean Sea and the West Indies.

This chart made it clear that it would be safe to place an embargo on further shipments of castor beans.

SUMMARY OF IMPORTS 1918
IN LONG TONS

SHEET NO.1		JAN.	FEB.	MAR.	APR.	MAY	JUNE	JULY	AUG.	SEPT.	OCT.	NOV.	DEC.
TOTAL	Requirements	1502M	3015M	4501M	5980M	7522M	9431M	10579M	11752M				
	Actual Deliveries	1513M	14.86M	1419M	1542M	1508M	1488M	1253M					
Ammonia	Requirements		1.2M	1.7M	2.3M	2.9M	3.4M	4M	4.6M	5M	5.7M	6.3M	6.9M
	Actual Deliveries	575											
Antimony Metal, Matte & Regulus	Requirements		1.3M	1.9M	2.4M	3.2M	3.8M	4.4M	5.1M	5.7M	6.3M	7M	7.6M
	Actual Deliveries	632											
Antimony – Ore	Requirements		0.8M	1.2M	1.6M	2M	2.5M	2.9M	3.3M	3.7M	4.1M	4.5M	5M
	Actual Deliveries	417											
Arsenic	Requirements		0.4M	0.6M	0.8M	1M	1.2M	1.4M	1.6M	1.8M	2M	2.2M	2.4M
	Actual Deliveries	204											
Asbestos	Requirements		16	24	32	40	48	56	64	72	80	88	96
	Actual Deliveries	8										Surplus to 7-20-1945	
Asphalt	Requirements		18M	27M	36M	45M	53M	62M	70M	79M	88M	97M	105M
	Actual Deliveries	14M	3.5M	9.4M	8.7M								
Bananas	Requirements		62M	9.3M	7.2M	15M	18.6M	21.7M	24.8M	27.9M	31.0M	34.1M	37.2M
	Actual Deliveries	31M											
Beans – Castor	Requirements		1.6M	2.5M	3.3M	4.1M	5M	5.8M	6.6M	7.5M	8.3M	9.1M	10M
	Actual Deliveries	83									Surplus to 7-31-1919		
Bismuth	Requirements		8	12	16	20	24	28	32	36	40	44	48
	Actual Deliveries	4								Surplus to 8-10-1919			

FIGURE 40. SUMMARY OF IMPORTS

This is the first of several sheets on which were listed all the commodities considered necessary to import. The first four commodities were very far behind schedule, while on three others the requirements for the year had not only been met but there was a considerable surplus.

At the top of this chart the total requirements and deliveries were shown and the heavy line indicated that at the end of July requirements had not only been met, but slightly exceeded. The light lines showed that in January and February the deliveries had been considerably short of requirements, but the assignment of vessels to specific tasks and the embargoes placed on unnecessary commodities brought in during March the amount required and in the 3 succeeding months more than were needed—the surplus just balancing the shortage for January and February.

It was clear at that time that there were more ships engaged in the import trade than were necessary and accordingly a large number of them were turned over to the army, with the result that in July there was only a slight surplus of imports. In other words, the Shipping Board was making progress in its task of bringing in the necessary imports with as few ships as possible.

of these commodities was shown on a separate chart. Figure 39 illustrates how the importation of castor beans stood on August 31. The requirements amounted to 10,000 long tons a year, or 883 per month, and when the chart was reproduced enough had been received to last at that rate until October of the following year. Accordingly, no further import licenses were issued for castor beans and the vessels coming in from the various trade regions carried other necessary commodities.

Summary of Imports

In order to present the import situation so that it could be grasped as a whole, all of the necessary commodities were listed alphabetically on a set of charts with the total at the top of the first sheet (see Figure 40). The first commodity, ammonia, was almost 7 months behind schedule, for although 575 tons were required per month, only about 100 tons had been received. Antimony metal was a month and a half behind the schedule, although some had been received every month as indicated by the light lines. Of the antimony ore only 2 months' supply had been received during the 7 months.

Although the requirements for bananas were 30,700 tons per month, in the first 7 months in 1918 enough had been imported to meet the requirements for a year and a half. The vessels engaged in this trade were large, swift, seaworthy, and equipped with refrigerator compartments and, therefore, ideal for carrying meat to the troops in France. The chart made it plain that these banana boats should be taken off the West Indies trade and assigned to the army for trans-Atlantic service.

At the top of this chart the total requirements and deliveries were shown and the heavy line indicated that at the end of July requirements had not only been met, but slightly exceeded. The light lines showed that in January and February the deliveries had been considerably short of requirements, but the assignment of vessels to specific tasks and the embargoes placed on unnecessary commodities brought in during March the amount required and in the three succeeding months more than was needed—the surplus just balancing the shortage for January and February. It was clear at that time that there were more ships engaged in the import trade than were necessary and accordingly a large number of them were turned over to the army with the result that in July there was only a slight surplus of imports. In other words, the Shipping Board was making progress in its task of bringing in the necessary imports with as few ships as possible.

Individual Trade Region Charts

In order to get better control over the cargoes carried, the world map was divided into 27 trade regions and for each region a set of charts was made up showing what commodities were required from that region, in what amounts, and the progress made in meeting the requirements. The chart of the East Asian region (see Figure 41) made it clear that at the end of July the imports were almost a month ahead of schedule and pointed out the shortages and oversupply of the various commodities.

When a ship was chartered for a voyage to any trade region, it was possible by consulting this chart to

NO.1 EAST ASIAN

IMPORTS IN LONG TONS

1918	JAN.	FEB.	MAR.	APR.	MAY	JUNE	JULY	AUG.	SEPT.	OCT.	NOV.	DEC.
Requirements of Desig. Imports	35M	75M	36M	148M	206M	265M	324M	383M				
Tons of Designated Imports	37M	37M	11M	37M	59M	59M						
Antimony, Metal												
Requirements		1.2M	1.8M	2.4M	3M	3.6M	4.2M	4.8M	5.4M	6M	6.6M	7.2M
Actual Deliveries	652											
Antimony, Ore												
Requirements		0.2M	0.3M	0.4M	0.5M	0.6M	0.7M	0.8M	0.9M	1M	1.1M	1.2M
Actual Deliveries	83											
Camphor												
Requirements		0.4M	0.6M	0.8M	1M	1.2M	1.4M	1.6M	1.8M	2M	2.2M	2.4M
Actual Deliveries	217											
Cocoanut Shells												
Requirements	0						0.9M					
Actual Deliveries												
Copal, Mauri & Damar												
Requirements		0.4M	0.6M	0.8M	1M	1.2M	1.4M	1.6M	1.8M	2M	2.2M	2.4M
Actual Deliveries	167											
Copper, Refined & Blister												
Requirements		0.4M	0.4M	0.8M	1.1M	1.4M	1.8M	2.1M	2.4M	2.3M	3M	3.4M
Actual Deliveries	225	150	50	333								
Copra												
Requirements		6.6M	1.0M	1.4M	1.7M	2.0M	2.4M	2.7M	3.1M	3.4M	3.7M	4.1M
Actual Deliveries	3.9M											
Cotton, Raw												
Requirements		0.5M	0.8M	1M	1.3M	1.5M	1.8M	2M	2.3M	2.5M	2.8M	3M
Actual Deliveries	250		74	425								
Graphite or Plumbago												
Requirements		0.5M	0.5M				No Requirements after March 31, 1918.			Surplus to Dec 1919		
Actual Deliveries	96	393	0									
Hides, Cattle												
Requirements		0.3M	0.8M	1.1M	1.7M		No Requirements after May 30, 1918.					
Actual Deliveries	103	167	501	369	523							

132

FIGURE 41. INDIVIDUAL TRADE CHART

There were charts for each of the 27 trade regions. They showed the progress made toward meeting the requirements from each region and served as a basis for the allocation of ships.

Although the total imports from the East Asian trade region were nearly a month ahead of schedule, most of the commodities wanted in small quantities were far behind. On "antimony ore," for instance, none had been received during the first 5 months and during June only slightly more than 1 month's supply; on "copal" only enough to meet the requirements for a month and a half had been received.

On "raw cotton," however, heavy shipments had come in; in fact, the receipts for 7 months equaled the requirements for 2 years.

On graphite and hides the receipts during the first few months were considered sufficient for the entire year. On the second sheet of this chart it was shown that heavy shipments had been received of silk, tea, and tin. These excess receipts overbalanced the shortages, so that, as is shown by the heavy line at the top of this chart, the receipts were a month and a half in excess of requirements. The importance of time and its relation to work is made clear in this chart.

SUMMARY OF TRADES 1918

IMPORTS IN LONG TONS

SHEET NO.1	JAN	FEB	MAR	APR	MAY	JUNE	JULY	AUG	SEPT	OCT	NOV	DEC
TOTAL												
Requirements of Designated Imports	1502M	3015M	4500M	5960M	7322M	9034M	10519M	11715M				
Actual Designated Imports		1513M	1486M	1479M	1542M	1509M	1498M	1255M				
1. East Asian												
Requirements	38M	37M	75M	111M	148M	205M	265M	324M	383M			
Actual Deliveries		37M	36M	37M	50M	53M						
2. East Indian												
Requirements	22M	44M	63M	81M	98M	115M	131M	147M	163M	179M	195M	
Actual Deliveries		19M	18M	16M								
3. British Indian												
Requirements	31M	31M	31M	122M	152M	180M	209M	236M				
Actual Deliveries		6M	31M	29M	50M	26M						
4. Australian												
Requirements	49M	50M	99M	147M	246M	296M	346M	358M	370M	362M	394M	406M
Actual Deliveries			43M			50M		12M				
5. Hawaiian												
Requirements	80M	160M	240M	320M	382M	444M	506M	563M				
Actual Deliveries					62M			59M				
6. Amazonian												
Requirements	2.5M	5M	7.5M	10M	13M	15M	18M	20M	23M	25M	28M	30M
Actual Deliveries												
7. Central Brazilian												
Requirements	66M	78M	144M	184M	249M	311M	367M	423M	469M	515M		
Actual Deliveries			40M	65M	62M	56M		46M				

134

FIGURE 42. SUMMARY OF TRADES

This chart showed the progress made by the United States Shipping Board in the operation of ships and presented a complicated situation in a clearer manner than would have been possible with words and figures. It served as a basis for the allocation of ships to those trades on which they were most needed.

On the East Asian trade during March, April, and May more tonnage had been received than was needed, and therefore vessels had been transferred from that trade to another with the result that less tonnage came in during June and July.

On the East Indian trade there had been a steady overdelivery, which was greater than ever during the last 3 months. The chart made it clear that when vessels returned from this trade, they should be assigned to another trade which was behind schedule.

advise the agents as to what commodities should be
brought back on her return trip.

Summary of Trades

The allocation of ships to the various trades was
the key to the successful handling of the import problem. A Summary of Trades Chart (see Figure 42)
was drawn to show how the requirements from all the
trade regions had been met. As was shown in Figure
41, the deliveries from the first trade region, East Asia,
were nearly a month ahead of schedule; the East Indian
deliveries were nearly 4 months ahead, and the
Hawaiian 3 months behind schedule. When a steamer
arrived in this country from Singapore, in the East
Indian region, the chart made it evident that she should
be allocated to the Australian or Hawaiian trade instead of being sent back to Singapore.

The line showing totals at the top of this chart advised those in charge of the allocation of ships whether
or not they could turn over more ships to the army for
the transportation of troops and supplies. It showed
how well their handling of the vessels controlled by the
Shipping Board met the import requirements. *A single line measured the service rendered by the entire
American Merchant Marine.*

These charts as used in the Shipping Board showed
the facts clearly and assembled those facts in such a
way that they pointed to definite action. But at the
same time they pointed clearly to the responsibility for
lack of action. In September, 1918, the sources of
information for the charts were shut off.

CHAPTER X

CONCLUSION

Facts in Their Relation to Time

The Gantt chart shows facts in their relation to time, emphasizing their movement through time, and therefore compels a man to take action based on the facts shown just as if he were responding to a force of motion.

The use of Gantt charts makes it necessary to have a plan; they compare what is done with what was planned; they show the reasons why performance falls short of the plan; they fix responsibility for the success or failure of a plan; they are remarkably compact; they are easy to draw and easy to read; they visualize the passing of time, and therefore help to reduce idleness and waste of time; they measure the momentum of industry.

Uses of the Various Gantt Charts

The Layout Chart helps to plan work so as to make the best possible use of the available men and machines and also so to arrange orders as to secure whatever deliveries may be desired within the capacity of the plant. The Load Chart keeps executives advised as to the amount of work ahead of the plant and enables them to co-ordinate workmen, equipment, processes, orders, and prices. The Progress Chart helps to get work done by showing a comparison of what is done with what should have been done and enables the executive to foresee future happenings with considerable accuracy. It shows the effect of past decisions and points out the action which should be taken in the future.

The Man and Machine Record Charts show whether management is good or bad:

1. Are the machines being run all day?
2. Are the men doing a full day's work?
3. If not, what are the reasons?

The answers to these questions are the ultimate facts in regard to the management of any manufacturing plant. If the men and machines are doing a full day's work, it is obvious that all the other details in the management of the plant are being taken care of on time. Shop orders, production cards, layout charts, and reports of all kinds are merely a part of the mechanism which leads up to or follows the Man and Machine Record Charts. They measure the service rendered by the workman, the foreman, and the management.

Each day when a man fails to do a fair day's work the reason is shown on a Man Record Chart. If that failure is due to absence, slowness, or avoidable mistakes, it is the fault of the workman, but if his failure is due to lack of instruction, to tool troubles, or to a machine in need of repairs, the fault is with the management. This chart, therefore, measures the service rendered by the individual workman and also the use the management makes of his service. The Machine Record Chart measures the ability of the management to make satisfactory use of the equipment at its disposal. The

Progress Chart shows how well the management is organized to get work done.

General Benefits of Gantt Charts

In the previous chapters Gantt charts have been shown as:

1. A simple and effective method of planning work.
2. A way of presenting facts so that they can be easily understood.
3. A means of eliminating idleness and waste.
4. A method of getting things done on time.

But Gantt charts stand for something more than that, for where they have been in use for some time one will find:

1. Machines and equipment in good condition.
2. Floor space arranged for use; neither cluttered up with unnecessary things nor arranged for appearance only.
3. Work moving rapidly from one operation to another without confusion.
4. Large reductions in inventories of raw materials, work in process, and finished goods, because of the shortening of manufacturing time.
5. Increased production—not through speeding up workmen but by removing the obstacles which prevent them from doing their best.
6. Reduced costs, because of the elimination of idleness and waste as well as improvements in processes.

7. Men in subordinate positions willing to shoulder responsibility instead of "passing the buck," because they have definite duties and clear-cut jobs.

8. Courage and initiative stimulated, because men know they will get fair play.

9. No favoritism or special privilege, because every man's record can be seen by others.

10. Satisfied workmen, because the delays over which they have no control are few and they are left free to do a full day's work and therefore earn better wages.

11. Poor workmen trained and developed until they make good.

12. Promotions going to men who know their jobs and, therefore, an organization being built up of men who "know what to do and how to do it."

13. Men interested in their work, not only because of the wages but because they have an opportunity to increase their knowledge and improve their skill.

Seeing such changes take place in one plant after another, watching arbitrary management become democratic and finding workmen not only interested in their work but proud of it, strengthens the conviction that *the Gantt chart is the most notable contribution to the art of management made in this generation.*

APPENDIX

APPENDIX A

HOW A MANAGER USES GANTT CHARTS

By Frank W. Trabold

Many years' experience as an executive in an industrial plant during which time I operated both with and without production and control charts convinces me that any executive operating without control charts of some satisfactory character in any plant that is more than a one-man proposition must of necessity be woefully ignorant of the actual conditions surrounding the work over which he has supervision. An executive without control charts can have but little idea of the potentialities in either sales or production, and when his operations show a profit it is usually because he is lucky enough to be in an industry where competition is not keen or to have an organization of subordinates of unusual ability.

Such a position is at best hazardous and a reliance on good luck may be disastrous. Eventually competition stiffens, and men are lost through one reason or another. A change in the financial control will almost invariably affect such an organization. Consolidations cause changes in departmental heads and their staffs are frequently disorganized, with a resultant chaos which is very difficult to correct and the true causes of which it is difficult even to discern. Where no control charts exist, straightening out processes are practically fresh starts without the value of previous experience being available.

One frequently hears from operating executives who do not use charts and do not "need" them certain comments on the futility of "getting in an efficiency man at the cost of several thousand dollars who did nothing except show a mass of charts indicating how poorly a good business was being run." I must confess that in my early days in operating a plant I too scoffed at these specialists whom I regarded as charlatans who through claims of superior knowledge drew down big, fat fees and went their way to the next gullible owner who would take them on long enough to find out he must finally place his dependence on his "tried and true" crew. Now, however, I know from experience that just as there are good and poor tool-makers, good and poor stenographers, good and poor foremen, good and poor floor-sweepers, and good and poor policies inaugurated by the high officials, so there are good and poor men engaged in the installation of production and control systems. Moreover, I know from years of operation, first with an entire absence of charts and then with a fairly good assortment of charts, that I would never again even hope to get along intelligently without them.

For years as a sales manager I had to wait every month for the report as to what time I could promise delivery, and this statement as a rule was not obtainable until about the tenth of the month covering conditions in the plant load as of the end of the preceding month. Usually accompanying this report would be a caution to exercise care in the use of this information, as in the time required to make it up conditions had so changed through the receipt of orders as to necessitate a further survey of the work ahead in the light of any promise which had to be kept. Better to have said the report was "no good" or, much better, to have saved the time and expense in preparing it at all simply because custom demanded that a positive delivery promise be furnished with each estimate given the sales department for quotation to customers. Frequently in periods of months these estimates averaged some 25 per day. Imagine the work involved in surveying the production possibilities of equipment 25 times per day, and imagine still further the utter lack of dependability in such promises when this work in a plant containing some 200 producing machines of various types was delegated to a single individual who besides this "promise" making had many other things to do! Still we went on—and profitably, but how profitably in comparison with the possibilities can somewhat be gaged by the fact that later, during the stress of the war period with all its varieties of causes retarding production, the actual production in all departments of the plant in question increased materially over pre-war periods.

The eventual installation of Gantt Load Charts showed always and instantly just how many days' work was assigned to each machine. If on July 1 a specific class of machine was shown to be loaded until September 15, it was obvious that no further work could be started until September 16. All orders were charted as they came in. By this means we avoided the giving of delivery promises out of all reason in comparison with what could be accomplished, nor were we longer subject to a sales department representative's inveigling a shop foreman into giving a promise that was impossible of performance without setting some other obligation aside. It permitted an intelligent promise to be promptly made and allowed correspondence, formerly held up for days while "working up a promise," to be promptly dispatched. As the charts were adjusted each week to cover the manufacturing contingencies constantly arising, and as blueprints were taken off and furnished to those concerned, the entire organization was kept acquainted with the current plant condition.

Furthermore, these charts always showed clearly and unmistakably work on which execution had failed; they made plain what classes of equipment were being loaded too far in the future for safety; guided policies as to the wisdom of taking on new customers; showed the expediency of overtime or night shifts; raised the question of proper equipment balance; and in case of low loads stimulated the sales activity. They also automatically prevented the jams which all uncharted shops are continually getting into, and by their use work was always charted in accordance with contract promise. For a given quantity and a given time, the estimated production time is charted. When charted the performance is gaged, and ordinarily accomplished.

Within the past year I attended a gathering of department heads of a plant in Chicago where a most interesting instance of the necessity for chart control developed. A certain forging called a "cutter head" had been sold on the basis of delivery of approximately 300 per day. The job was easy of accomplishment by the forging department, but the contract provided for a machine operation, and only through the desire of a conscientious department head to seek relief was it disclosed that the machine equipment available could produce no more than some 70 per day. For months the customer complained, the sales department "kept after" the shop, and the shop promised to do better. Of course, it is plain that all the operations should have been investigated in the first instance, but they were not. If charting had prevailed in this plant, the inability to meet the service required would have been apparent before starting the job, merely through the plain fact that 300 could not be squeezed into a 70 line.

My first real respect for outside chart men was born when it was proved to me beyond a doubt that the idleness of the equipment in a plant under my supervision was three times as great as I believed it to be, and this at a time when work was booked for many months ahead of each machine. It was a distinct shock not only to find the extent of this idleness but to note the causes shown on the chart, most of which could be easily eliminated when known. These charts provided an excellent basis for greater productivity of the equipment. An account of a few of these causes, with the means of correction and consequent elimination of the idleness, will perhaps be of interest.

Every week some new phase of idleness was disclosed by the charts and quickly brought under control, whereas until charted it had existed for many years unnoticed. I recall an instance when the charts showed an excessive amount of idleness due to repairs. An investigation showed that these repairs were on pumps on milling machines, and when this fact was brought in its magnitude to the attention of the superintendent it was quickly corrected by a simple mechanical means which practically eliminated the idleness through removing the cause. One hundred dollars per week would be a modest estimate as the saving in this one case. I have seen idleness costing hundreds of dollars per week almost entirely eliminated by a foreman who confessed it was "easier to keep the equipment going than keep explaining why it was idle." The department of which he was the head had for years been the "neck of the bottle," in which jams occurred, and which frequently had to go on overtime or night shifts to catch up.

Idleness of machinery of another class to the extent of many hours per week was caused by an old rule that the machines must be oiled each day before the afternoon shift was started. This work took a man about an hour, during which time the machines stood idle. The average of half an hour for each of these machines per day for this purpose was tolerated for years, and yet the remedy was simply to shift the lunch period of two men half an hour ahead and have this oiling done during the regular lunch shutdown. Of course, the original arrangement should never have been made or allowed to exist; but it did exist, as did many other things disclosed by these charts.

Among other things I have seen an unusual amount of idleness disclosed because of "no help" when discussion with the employment manager developed the fact that he relied upon men passing the plant and seeing the "Help Wanted" sign, whereas when $3 was spent in local newspaper advertising it brought many times the number of applicants that could be hired. This experience also emphasized the necessity for an employment manager versed in shop conditions and operations, and showed the necessity for some supervision of the employed men, especially the new ones. In a certain case an advertisement was inserted for a "broacher" and no responses developed. While it was true that what was wanted was a man for a broaching machine, the work really called only for a careful man who could be instructed properly and sufficiently in 30 minutes. In another case an advertisement called for "trimmers," when men were wanted for presses for trimming flash from forgings. The applicants were wood-trimmers, clothing-makers of a branch called "trimmers," trimmers of men's hats, and milliners.

Beyond the "unearned burden," the expense of idle equipment is still more costly and often the pay of the operator goes on just the same. If the delay is caused by a repair which can be made in an hour, the operator stands around doing nothing. Loss of possible profits in the work not performed is another factor making for expense of idleness.

Many machines in shops have a burden rate of several times the wage rate for operating them. It seems wise, then, if we consider it necessary to put a man on a time-clock schedule in order to see that he gets in on time and does not leave until quitting time, that we provide a similar means for knowing whether our machines are actually operating during the hours the power and supervision expense is being borne for their operation. From my own experience I know that the installation of idle machine charts provides a means of substantially increasing output.

With the installation of Man Record Charts I have found that some men who for years had reputations as stars really proved such, but others with similar reputations consistently failed to approach the standards set. On the other hand, men who for years were unnoticed and had passed as ordinary workmen proved exceptional in consistently high production performance. In too many manufacturing departments, as in other branches of business, the "good fellows" get the high rates, and this morale-disturbing practice goes on until some means is provided for measuring ability. Men who know themselves to be producing more each day than a fellow-worker who is getting a higher rate soon become disgruntled, and develop a grouch against the foreman for playing favorites and against the company for retaining the foreman. On the other hand, the fellow getting the high rate has little respect either for the foreman or the company because he knows he is "putting something over." No one gains, everyone loses, because there exists no means of knowing exactly how the various men measure up.

Piece work is somewhat different, but here also one finds much complaint because of certain favorites getting the best jobs. Load charts laid out, with each job to be done in its proper turn, eliminate the practice of favoritism; unless, indeed, the charts are disregarded by the foreman, in which case evasion of the proper sequence of jobs is quickly noticeable.

Charts of this general character lighten materially the load on an executive, in that after the work is charted only such items as fail to come through on time or fail to measure up to standard require attention. Without charts an executive must necessarily be moving about, incessantly watching everything in order to catch the few items requiring attention, the result being a general and constant supervision rather than an application of corrective work just where it is needed.

Charts remove much friction between the sales force and the shop, as by means of charts responsibility is quickly and justly placed and broken promises are quickly brought to light. The men are greatly influenced by the mere existence of these charts. The old methods of awaiting the arrival of costs to show a loss on account of poor production, the investigation of which seldom does any substantial good because of the long-elapsed period between its execution and the discovery of failure, should in these days be entirely done away with, and that shop is indeed unfortunate which continues to operate in the old way.

I have frequently seen charts bring up an average accomplishment to a standard previously thought impossible and within a comparatively short time justify an intelligent raising of the standard without creating any friction. Charts viewed daily admit of an examination of the entire operation; absence of charts permits an observation of just that proportion of the operation which an executive can keep actual watch over. Without charts an executive is utterly helpless and at the mercy of those on whom he depends for his departmental work. On the other hand, a daily supervision of the charts, with proper action taken on the necessities for action thus disclosed, will automatically insure a proper operating statement. If charts are used the arrival of the operating statement need not be anticipated with alarm.

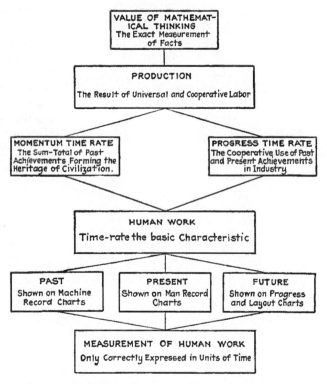

FIGURE 43. GRAPHIC BRIEF OF DEVELOPMENT OF SUBJECT
MATTER IN "THE MEASUREMENT OF HUMAN WORK"

APPENDIX B

THE MEASUREMENT OF HUMAN WORK

By Walter N. Polakov

The fundamental distinction between arts and sciences is that the latter are evolved from sharp, complete, and precise definitions of phenomena and their relations, while arts are based chiefly on "senses" not capable of precise definition. Science therefore permits exact measurement of what we call "facts," whereas in the arts the correctness of a didactic conclusion depends on the quality of thinking employed, and it may be accepted as correct only when it is arrived at by a strictly mathematical method of reasoning.

In the field of engineering this distinction is rather astonishing. Engineering has been defined as the science and art of directing the sources of power in nature for the use and well-being of mankind. Those branches which have been studied with the aid of mathematics have become branches of applied science; for instance, mechanical and electrical engineering, chemistry, etc. However, in that branch of engineering which deals with human forces, known as "management engineering," there has been until recently an almost complete absence of mathematical thinking, with the result that, instead of accurate measurement, we find vagueness, inadequacy, and looseness of reasoning.

The recent movement known as "scientific management" claims at least one characteristic of the scientific method—that of measurement with an accuracy and completeness unknown in industry even a score of years ago. Let us inquire into the methods and more particularly the units of measurement employed.

In the foreword to F. W. Taylor's "Shop Management," Henry R. Towne states:

> The monogram of our national initials, which is the symbol for our monetary unit, the dollar, is almost as frequently conjoined to the figures of an engineer's calculations as are the symbols

> indicating feet, minutes, pounds or gallons. The final issue . . . resolves itself into a question of dollars and cents . . . The *dollar* is the final term in almost every equation which arises in the practice of engineering . . .

and finally he remarks:

> I avail of these quotations to emphasize the fact that industrial engineering, of which shop management is an integral and vital part, implies not merely the making of a given product, but the making of that product at the *lowest cost* consistent with the maintenance of the intended standard of quality.

Stated in the words of another engineer, H. L. Gantt:

> The aim of our efficiency has not been to produce goods, but to harvest dollars. . . The production of goods was always secondary to the securing of dollars.

The dollar has been used improperly as the unit for measuring production. It cannot measure human work for two reasons: First, because its magnitude is variable. It diminishes in value as the productivity per hour of human work increases. The cost of living, as expressed in terms of money, has increased throughout the history of economic development. Second, the dollar does not imply time. A man working for a dollar per hour may produce more or less during that hour, and a man working for a dollar per piece may produce a piece in more or less time than an hour.

Whether the unit is suitable for measurement, clearly depends upon whether or not it is of the same dimensionality as the quantity to be measured. This is the core of our inquiry. If we are examining lines we measure them in lineal units (inches, feet, yards, miles, etc.); if we are concerned with surfaces, we use square units (square inches, square yards, acres, etc.). What are we dealing with in production or, stated more accurately, what is the common attribute or characteristic of production which is necessary and sufficient to distinguish it from any other activity, and how can it be measured? In other words, what is the *dimensionality of production?* Upon the correct answer to this question depends the selection of the proper unit for measuring production.

Production may be defined as *human work organized on the co-operation of living and dead men for the conscious purpose of*

changing the form of matter or the direction or character of force.
The outstanding factor in production is human work. That distinguishes production from any other activity. It is human, and
therefore, a logarithmic function of time which defines the human
dimension. It is also work. A definition of work is given by
R. H. Smith, Professor Emeritus of Birmingham University:

> Force itself is a time rate, namely, that of transference of
> momentum; and thus work done, which is of the same dimension
> as energy, is
>
> $$\frac{\text{Momentum}}{\text{Time}} \times \text{Distance}$$

To take a concrete example: The momentum of a locomotive
divided by time gives its rate per hour, but it must cover distance
before it becomes work.

What is meant by the phrase in our definition of production
"co-operation of living and dead men?" Living men apply their
knowledge and energy to work, but by far the greater part of their
knowledge has not originated with them. It has been handed down
from men who lived long ago. The machines or tools which living
men use have been invented, designed, and even built largely by
men who are no longer living. The construction of a locomotive,
for instance, involves the work of geometricians back to Euclid, of
the philosophers who created calculus, of chemists, metallurgists,
and so forth. In fact, a great deal more has been done toward
building a locomotive before the living man begins work on the
first piece of steel that goes into it than is done during its actual
construction.

This co-operation of living and dead men creates all our material, intellectual, and spiritual wealth. Before we begin any work
we have at our disposal sciences, knowledge, machinery, materials,
ideals, methods—all created and handed down by those who worked
before us. It is our part to bring to the work our energy and
the ability to co-ordinate and apply what we have received from
preceding generations and thus by means of our time-binding energy
to create further material, intellectual, and spiritual wealth.

It is apparent, then, that the human work done is a product
of two time rates: one the momentum of civilization, transferred

from generation to generation, where the time element appears as an exponent; another the velocity or motion time rate of contemporary human beings performing the work. Inasmuch as during the life of an individual, even from day to day, a progress of accumulation of experience, knowledge, skill, etc., is being made, the rate of progress is also an exponential function of time.

Coming back to our definition of production as *human work organized on the co-operation of living and dead men for the conscious purpose of changing the form of matter or the direction or character of force,* this sharply distinguishes production from animal effort, physical occurrence, individual discovery, disorganized conflicting effort, or activity independent of results accomplished by past generations of men. In the light of this definition and its significant limitations let us again ask the question: What is the dimensionality of production? The answer is now obvious: It is—*time.* Time is the attribute or characteristic which is present in all production in industry and is susceptible to uniform measurement. The inappropriateness of the dollar as a unit of measure is again confirmed. The blunder of confusing dimensions and expressing time in such units as weight, length, volume, etc., is likewise evident. None of these are of the same dimension as the quantity measured and therefore they cannot express the effect of the utilization of knowledge, experience, and co-operative effort for the well-being of man.

In nature it does not matter how long it takes to convert a mass of ferns into anthracite, or how much time elapses while the mighty river digs its bed; but for man, conscious of time and limited to the length of time he can live, it makes a cardinal difference how long it takes to accomplish a piece of work. Again quoting Professor Smith:

> The life of man and of generations of men is short, and ever since we emerged from the luxuries of the Euphrates Valley and more especially since we created the United States of America, the time element has been the chief domineering factor in industrial and commercial life.

Time being the specific dimension of man and of production, the units of time are thus the only units by which production can be measured. Any theory in regard to mankind in which time is considered of no consequence is utterly useless in our practical life or industrial world.   In considering transportation we deal in miles per *hour;* in power production we reckon with pounds of steam per hour or kilowatts per *hour;* in production we deal with output per *hour.*

The practical task of controlling production must of necessity begin with measurement and, to be correct, measurements must be made in the proper dimension.   It would be a grave blunder to apply a unit of one dimension to an entirely different dimension or to use a measurement which contains a variable element.   We cannot use for measuring human work the units of mechanical power such as foot-pounds or horse-power which embrace only the muscular work of men, even though these expressions contain the time rate, for it would be a confusion of part with the whole.   The time rate of man's work is the only measure of production which is of the same dimensionality as the energy causing it and it is as constant as the solar system itself.

The Gantt graphic method of controlling production, that is, the management of human work, is the only method ever presented which is based on a correct unit of measurement.   The productive time rate is a prerequisite in the use of the Gantt methods.   In the instructions for the use of Gantt charts in the Ordnance Department, United States Army, the first caption reads:

TIME; THE ONE CONSTANT IS TIME

The amount to be done in the time unit is always represented by the same length of line.   Any chart may, therefore, have many scales on it.

Since time may be spent for different purposes and the amounts of work that can be done in a unit of time may differ of necessity, the scales may be as varied as are the human activities themselves, but we cannot conceive human activity without or beyond time.

Time in its relation to our existence is divided into present, past, and future.   Consciously or unconsciously, Gantt developed his mechanism of production control so as to enable us to visualize the use made of time in its present, past, and future aspects.   Hence we have three fundamental managerial problems visualized in three forms of charts: applied to the present or to current work—Man Record Charts; referred to work done in the past—Machine Record Charts; and finally, projected to future work—Progress Charts with their schedules laid out on the time scale of future requirements.

During the time devoted to productive work there is a variable amount of work done, and this is what is shown on the Man Record Chart, but this work is performed and directed by men. "To feel the lure of perfection," says Professor C. J. Keyser, "in one or more types of excellence, however lowly, is to be human; not to feel it is to be sub-human." And a chart of this kind involves that ideal of service. It shows what is expected to be accomplished within the work time for any occupation, however lowly.

In such a chart this ever-striving impulse of self-expression in service which throbs in every human being is given adequate expression and stimulus. It is accomplished by predetermining the ideal, however modest, which is accepted by a man as within his power of attainment. Then, and only then, can the lines of attainment be drawn from day to day to denote the falling short of the aim or equaling and even surpassing it, as the obstacles of inertia, ignorance, or lack of co-ordination are overcome by the strongest of all human propensities—the desire to excel oneself. This type of chart can truthfully be called a tool for humanizing industry, for it not only reveals to a man his own dignity and capacity as a creator, but subtly, though persistently, calls for co-operation between the workers with brain and brawn. It tells what each of us and all of us are doing at present.

The Machine Record Chart reveals to one who reads between the lines much more than merely the time a certain machine was idle. Its scale is also time, but the time during which a machine remains unproductive has a graver significance than a reminder that "time is money." It means that someone, who should have operated it or supervised its operation, did no work and the time of inventing, developing, and building this machine, which is greater in its productive significance than the time of the operator, is irretrievably lost.

Likewise, the Material Utilization Chart (like that of fuel utilization developed by the author) indicating the waste of material

or energy, has a deeper meaning.[1] It shows the extent to which the
work of other men in recovering, preparing, and delivering this
material or energy has been destroyed. It means that the work of
hosts of other men has been rendered useless and their productive
time forever lost. This type of chart gives us the measure of our
utilization of work that has been done before. It proves whether
we are worthy of our inheritance from the *past*.

Lastly, the Progress Chart integrates all elements of work.
It sums up the progress made, its acceleration, its retardation, its
time rate. Like other charts, it brings together the ideal and the
fact. Its ideal projects into the future and sets before us the task
which we are called on to perform, no matter how small or how
great it may be—whether filling an order in a shop, feeding a
nation, or advancing the life and happiness of mankind. It calls
for a plan and vision of the *future*. It is based on knowledge of
the past and it reveals our position at present.

This time concept in the control of industry, direction of production, and measurement of human work thus stands revealed as the
wished-for solution, free from error of confused types and dimensions. It refers all facts to the irreducible and final element of
human life—time. Because it is true to the human dimension, it
is both human and humane; hence it obliterates conflicts between
men and management, promotes the fullest exercise of man's creative
forces, and places work in its proper relation to life.

[1] See Walter N. Polakov, "Mastering Power Production," Engineering Magazine
Co., 1921.

Printed in the USA
CPSIA information can be obtained
at www.ICGtesting.com
CBHW020405220124
3647CB00008B/710